PRETRIB

Also by Alan E. Kurschner

Prewrath: A Very Short Introduction to the Great Tribulation, Rapture, and Day of the Lord

Antichrist Before the Day of the Lord: What Every Christian Needs to Know about the Return of Christ

For many free online resources, visit us at AlanKurschner.com

PRETRIB

Examining the Foundations of
Pretribulation Rapture Theology

ALAN E. KURSCHNER

Eschatos Publishing
P.O. Box 747
Rice Lake, WI 54868

Printed in the United States of America

Publisher's Cataloging-in-Publication Data

Kurschner, Alan E., author.
Pretrib : examining the foundations of pretribulation Rapture theology / Alan E. Kurschner.
Rice Lake, WI : Eschatos Publishing, 2022. | Also available in audiobook format. | Includes bibliographical references and index.
LCCN 2022907583 (print) | ISBN 978-0-9853633-9-0 (paperback) | ISBN 979-8-9861572-0-7 (ebook)
LCSH: Rapture (Christian eschatology) | Bible--Prophecies. | Prophecy--Christianity. | Dispensationalism. | Bible. Daniel, IX, 24-27--Prophecies. | BISAC: RELIGION / Christian Theology / Eschatology. | RELIGION / Biblical Studies / Prophecy. | RELIGION / Biblical Commentary / General.
LCC BT887 .K87 2022 (print) | LCC BT887 (ebook) | DDC 236/.9--dc23.

For online resources, visit AlanKurschner.com

Cover Design by M. S. Corley
Interrior Layout Design by Uberwriters LLC.
www.uberwriters.com

Acknowledgments

This book is dedicated to Robert and Judy Van Kampen. Robert Van Kampen pioneered prewrath premillennial eschatology, articulating a more accurate biblical picture of our Lord's future return. His wife, Judy, undoubtedly sacrificed many hours as he researched and wrote. In addition, their hearts for spreading the gospel through missions have produced immeasurable fruit in the body of Christ. For these reasons, I gladly dedicate this book to them.

I also want to thank the following individuals for reading, reviewing, and proofing the manuscript in part, or in whole: my editor Heidi Tolliver-Walker; layout editor Hilton Rahme; and the following readers: Barry Horner, Alan Hultberg, Charles Cooper, Chris White, Dave and Mo Dardinger, Michael Coldagelli, Ryan Habbena, Greg Anderson, Zachary Dawson, and Travis Snow.

I also thank my wife, Donna, for her support, and for the prayers from many who follow Eschatos Ministries. I could not predict the day nor hour of this book's publication, but I hope that it was worth the wait. I will let the readers of this volume judge for themselves whether that is the case.

Contents

Illustrations

Tables

Introduction

PRETRIBULATION RAPTURE THEOLOGY

In this introduction, I will first outline the two foundations of pretribulation theology, followed by a sketch of the history of this view. I will then explain why this book matters.

This book focuses on the two major foundations of pretribulation theology or what I am calling the *ecclesiastical* presupposition and the *Parousia* presupposition. In Part 1, I will examine the ecclesiastical presupposition. This presupposition is referred to as "ecclesiastical" because how one understands the relationship between the church and Israel will influence one's interpretation of specific eschatological passages such as, for instance, the Olivet Discourse, Paul's Thessalonian letters, and the book of Revelation. Pretribulation eschatology contends that there will be a seven-year interim (or to use their term, "Tribulation period") that will take place between the present church age and the millennium.[1] During this period, traditional pretribulationism maintains that God works only with Israel and not the church. Therefore, it infers that the church must

---

1. Cf. Blaising and Bock, *Progressive Dispensationalism*, 317; Showers, *Pre-Wrath Rapture View*, 12–17.

be raptured before God resumes his program with Israel. Chapter 1 will situate this foundational belief within the larger theology of dispensationalism, sketching its history and distinctives. Chapter 2 will focus on the pretribulation interpretation of Daniel's seventy weeks prophecy found in Dan 9:24–27, the main *traditional* dispensational proof text for pretribulationism. Chapter 3 will hone in on this presupposition, addressing the major belief of traditional dispensationalism that God does not work with Israel and the church simultaneously.

In Part 2, I will examine the Parousia presupposition, the foundational premise that disconnects the rapture from the second coming.[2] While the ecclesiastical presupposition creates the foundational criterion for traditional pretribulationism concerning Israel and the church, the Parousia presupposition establishes a hermenuetical principle regarding the relationship between the rapture and the second coming. In the pretribulation framework, the rapture is disconnected from the second coming by Daniel's seventieth week, which they consider to be coextensive with God's wrath.[3] In Part 2, I will argue that, in fact, the rapture belongs to the second coming and that the second coming is a unified extended-whole of events. Chapter 4 will describe key terms that the New Testament authors used to describe this extended, glorious event. Chapter 5 will critique several of pretribulationism's supposed "contrasts" that characterize a dichotomy between the rapture and the second coming. Chapter 6 will argue that the second coming does not begin

2. Because the Greek term *parousia* refers not just to an arrival but also to a continuing presence (BDAG), the word is often used, particularly in scholarly circles, to refer to the whole event itself—the Parousia event.

3. E.g. Feinberg, *Case for the Pretribulation Rapture*, 58. Some pretribulationists posit a gap of time of days, weeks, months, or even years between the rapture and the beginning of the seven-year period. I will respond to this "gap interpretation" in Part 2.

with the battle of Armageddon. Chapter 7 will contend that the second coming begins with the rapture, thereby eliminating the possibility of a gap between the two events. To be sure, the rapture is not equated with the second coming (as posttribulationists believe). Instead, the rapture is one of the first events that will occur within the unified extended Parousia event. The rapture and God's wrath will occur back to back when Jesus returns.

Pretribulationism infers from these presuppositions that the rapture is signless and unannounced. They argue that the Bible does not predict any intervening prophetic events that will occur before the rapture; hence, it can happen "at any moment." If a single predicted event occurs before the rapture, it is believed, then Christ's return can no longer be considered imminent. Pretribulationists hold that the Bible does not prophesy a single sign or event that *must* occur before the rapture. Some events, they would say, *may* happen before the rapture (e.g. the reestablishment of the nation of Israel), but no predicted events *must* happen. The rapture of the church, therefore, is not conditional upon any signs or events. They believe that Christ can return today, this hour, or in the next moment.

This book also includes two appendices: (1) a brief explanation of the prewrath view, and (2) an outline of church mysteries that extend into the seventieth week of Daniel. There is a Scripture index for those searching for commentary on specific biblical passages. Bibliographic citations referenced in the footnotes are in short form, so the reader should consult the bibliography for full publication data. The definitions of Greek and Hebrew terms in this book are from the following standard lexicons:

(BDAG) *A Greek-English Lexicon of the New Testament and Other Early Christian Literature*. 3rd ed. Frederick W. Danker, Walter Bauer, William F. Arndt, and F. Wilbur Gingrich Chicago: University of Chicago Press, 2000.

(LN) *Greek-English Lexicon of the New Testament Based on Semantic Domains*. J. P. Louw and E. A. Nida. 2 vols. New York: United Bible Societies, 1988.

(HALOT) *The Hebrew and Aramaic Lexicon of the Old Testament*. Ludwig Koehler, Walter Baumgartner, and Johann J. Stamm. Translated and edited under the supervision of Mervyn E. J. Richardson. 4 vols. Leiden: Brill, 1994–1999.

A Sketch of Pretribulationism

Pretribulationism is a relatively new British-American view, promulgated by the nineteenth century Plymouth Brethren theologian John Nelson Darby (d. 1882).[4] If pretribulationism is found in other parts of the world today, it is because it has been exported by American and British pretribulational missionaries.

Darby made a sharp redemptive and spatial distinction between two peoples of God—"heavenly" (the church) and "earthly" (Israel) entities.[5] This would eventually be modified later in dispensationalism as the "church" and "Israel."[6] In 1864, S. P. Tregelles responded to Darby's dispensationalism and "signless" rapture theory with a litany of biblical objections in a concise yet influential book, *The Hope of Christ's Second Coming*. Using the framework created by Darby, dispensationalists continued to claim that because Israel had rejected her Messiah, God postponed the messianic kingdom prophecies for the future millennium kingdom. In the present dispensation of grace, which is essentially a "parenthesis" between Israel and the future millennial kingdom, God is working through the church. When Jesus returns, God's attention will be on Israel

4. Reiter, "History," 12.

5. Darby, *Collected Writings*, 11:41–54, 118–67; cf. Chafer, *Systematic Theology*, 1:xiv; 4:47.

6. Blaising, "Search for Definition," 24–25.

once again. Jesus, then, can come at any moment *for* his church, and seven years later, he will come *with* his church.[7]

In the latter part of the nineteenth century, the annual Niagara Bible Conference played a large role in promoting premillennialism, as well as pretribulationism.[8] During this time, there were three major figures within pretribulationism: James H. Brookes (1830–1897), C. I. Scofield (1843–1921), and A. C. Gaebelein (1861–1945). Robert Cameron, one of several speakers who opposed the rise of pretribulationism, described the conference environment as follows: "At the 1884 Conference it came to be the 'fashion' of every speaker to 'ring the changes' on the possibility of Christ's Coming any moment—before the morning dawned, before the meeting closed, and even before the speaker had completed his address."[9] The Niagara Bible Conference dissolved after 1900; however, Gaebelein founded an offshoot conference in Sea Cliff, New York, that met from 1901–1911. The Sea Cliff Bible Conference promulgated pretribulational imminence theology on a new level, supplemented by the magazine *Our Hope,* founded by Gaebelein.[10]

The whole period was formative for pretribulationism. Larry Pettegrew, commenting on the rapture debate between pretribulation and posttribulation Niagara teachers, observed: "The rapture, though taught primarily as pretribulational, had not been thought through carefully by many premillennialists up to that time. . . . The doctrine

7. These traditional dispensational notions will be described further in Chapter 1.

8. For a brief history, see Pettegrew, "Niagara Bible Conference," 331–47.

9. Pettegrew, "Niagara Bible Conference," 337. Even though the pretribulation sense of imminence eventually dominated the conferences, there was not always unanimity in the precise definition of imminence (see Reiter, "History of the Development of the Rapture Positions," 14).

10. Pettegrew, "Niagara Bible Conference," 343.

of imminency [eventually] was clarified and became a strong argument for pretribulationism."[11] Gaebelein encouraged Scofield to write the notes for what would become the most influential dispensational publication, the *Scofield Reference Bible*, unequaled in influence in its theology during the first half of the twentieth century and beyond.[12] The *Scofield Reference Bible* established the understanding of an imminent return of Jesus as a household belief in many theological circles in Britain and America. From that matrix, the second half of the twentieth century produced a trilogy of pretribulation publications: *The Rapture Question* (1957) by John F. Walvoord, *Things to Come* (1958) by J. Dwight Pentecost, and *Dispensationalism Today* (1965) by Charles C. Ryrie. These were followed by a trilogy of popular works: *The Late Great Planet Earth* (1970) by Hal Lindsey, the film *A Thief in the Night* (1972), and the ubiquitous Left Behind novel series (1995–2007) by Tim LaHaye and Jerry B. Jenkins, including its obligatory spin-offs.

Why This Book Matters

The thesis of this book is that a pretribulation, imminent rapture can no longer be maintained. Since it cannot be maintained, the implication of the critique in this book is clear: It establishes key prophecies that the church will witness before the rapture takes place (Joel 2:30–31, Mal 4:5, 1 Thess 5:2–3, 2 Thess 2:1–4). I have friends who are pretribulationists. While this book is a critique of their rapture theology, I have no ill will toward any of my brothers and sisters who hold to this view. I love them, and for this reason, I have written this book. We should desire to better understand this matter of the Lord's return. The answer to

11. Pettegrew, "Niagara Bible Conference," 347.
12. See Mangum and Sweetnam, *The Scofield Bible.*

the question of how many angels can dance on the head of a needle does not matter to our spiritual life. The question whether the last generation of the church will face the Antichrist's horrible persecution, however, does matter, and it matters greatly. How one sides on this question will impact how the Christian prepares—or does not prepare—for the most difficult times coming on the universal church. Jesus and the biblical authors taught that biblical expectancy results in a three-fold character: spiritual vigilance, longing hope, and discerning signs. If Christians practice these three strands of expectancy, they will rightly fulfill the Lord's instruction on how to watch for his delayed return. Practicing the proper expectancy of Jesus's return will substantially change the way we conceive and prepare for the Antichrist's great tribulation that awaits the final generation. That generation could very well be ours.

Conclusion

The introduction described the foundations of pretribulation rapture theology and the thesis of the book. It also described a historical sketch of pretribulationism and explained why this critique of pretribulation theology matters. Now we turn to Part 1, where I will examine the foundational presupposition in traditional pretribulation theology: the notion that God does not work with Israel and the church simultaneously. Chapter 1 will elaborate on the history and nature of dispensational theology. Chapter 2 will analyze the foundational proof text for pretribulationism: Daniel 9:24–27. Chapter 3 will critique the pretribulation belief that God does not work with Israel and the church simultaneously.

Part 1

THE ECCLESIASTICAL PRESUPPOSITION: GOD DOES NOT WORK WITH THE CHURCH AND ISRAEL SIMULTANEOUSLY

In Part 1, I will critique the first of two major foundations of pretribulation theology: the ecclesiastical presupposition. I describe it as "ecclesiastical" because, for traditional dispensationalism, the foundational argument for pretribulationism is a sharp distinction between Israel and the church. This view argues for an absolute dispensational change from God's purposes for the church in this present age to his purposes for Israel during Daniel's seventieth week.[1] John F. Walvoord, a noted pretribulationist, once claimed that pretribulationism is based on an inference of an ecclesiastical understanding between national Israel and the church: "[T]he rapture question is determined more by ecclesiology than eschatology."[2] Craig Blaising, a progressive dispensationalist, captures this traditional dispensational programmatic hermeneutic:

1. I will comment below on the prophecy of the seventieth week of Daniel.

2. Walvoord, *The Rapture Question,* 1st ed., 50.

> In much of this thinking, the pretribulational rapture was a systemic feature of dispensational theology tied directly to ecclesiology . . . . The church, as a previously unrevealed heavenly program, comes into existence as a parenthesis within the earthly program of God's purpose for Israel. This parenthesis must be closed for the earthly program to resume. The closure of that parenthesis is the pretribulational rapture. . . . Daniel's chronology of the seventy sevens, having been interrupted by the church, would resume. . . . the church by definition cannot be present when Daniel's "earthly" [Israel's] chronology resumes [emphasis his].[3]

It is not a bad practice to ground one's theology on inferences. For example, Jesus being worshipped implies his divinity (e.g. Rev 5:12–14). However, if an inference is based on a false premise, then the resulting theology is skewed and unsound. In Part 1, I will argue that the pretribulation ecclesiastical premise lacks biblical support. I will contend that God works with both the church and Israel simultaneously. This conclusion establishes that since God works with Israel and the church simultaneously now, it invalidates the theological principle that he will not work with them during the seventieth week.

Chapter 1 will relate the ecclesiastical presupposition to the theology of dispensationalism, sketching its history and distinctives. Chapter 2 will focus on the traditional pretribulation argument, which understands Daniel's prophecy in Dan 9:24–27 to exclude the church from existing on earth during this time. Chapter 3 will examine the traditional dispensational understanding that God did not work simultaneously with Israel and the church in the past; he does not work with Israel and the church in the present; and he will not work with Israel and the church during the seventieth week.

---

3. Blaising, "Case for the Pretribulation Rapture," 69.

Chapter 1

DESCRIPTIONS OF DISPENSATIONALISM

I affirm a futurist, premillennial, prewrath perspective. Prewrath eschatology shares several beliefs with pretribulationism: (1) key biblical events will be fulfilled in the future—e.g. from the Olivet Discourse and the book of Revelation, (2) a premillennial theology of the physical millennial kingdom waits to be established at Jesus's return, (3) God promises to restore national, ethnic Israel to their land,[1] and (4) the saints are promised exemption from the day of the Lord's wrath (cf. 1 Thess 5:9).[2] Unlike the pretribulation view, however, prewrath holds that the rapture and the resurrection will occur *sometime during the second half of Daniel's seven-year period.* Prewrath theology distinguishes between the Antichrist's great tribulation and the day of the Lord's wrath, a distinction that pretribulationism fails to recognize.[3] The Antichrist's great

1. See Porter and Kurschner, eds., *The Future Restoration of Israel.*

2. Cf. Rosenthal, *Pre-Wrath Rapture*, 116; Feinberg, "Case for the Pretribulation Rapture," 50–51.

3. E.g. Pretribulation theologian Gerald B. Stanton ("Doctrine of Imminency," 223) states, "We believe that the Bible teaches clearly

tribulation will be directed against God's saints until it is cut short with the coming of Jesus for the resurrection and rapture.[4] On that day, God will immediately begin to pour out his day-of-the-Lord wrath against the world. This distinction is critical to a proper understanding of eschatology. Failure to recognize this distinction conflates the two events. Pretribulation interpreters believe that the seven-year period is entirely God's wrath.[5] Thus, while "the Tribulation" is a commonly used term even among academics, I prefer to use the neutral biblical expression *Daniel's seventieth week* or *seven-year period.*

I have made these comments on prewrath eschatology at the outset so the reader is aware of my eschatological perspective. For further reading on the prewrath position, see Appendix 1, "A Brief Explanation of the Prewrath View."[6]

Most pretribulationists hold to the theological system of dispensationalism.[7] This system has gone through three

---

that the rapture will take place before the great tribulation, the time of the outpoured wrath of God." Similarly, John MacArthur ("Is Christ's Return Imminent?," 15) fails to make this distinction when he states, "God did not appoint us to wrath. The day of wrath that shall come in the Tribulation is not what we are to be preparing for."

4. The term "saints" (*hagios*) is a favorite of the apostle Paul to describe members of the church, meaning, "being dedicated or consecrated to the service of God" (BDAG; e.g. Rom 1:7, 1 Cor 1:2, Eph 1:1, Phil 1:1, Col 1:2). For example, Paul, recalling his days when he persecuted the church, describes the *church as saints*; compare Phil 3:6 with Acts 26:10. John in the book of Revelation uses this term as well, especially as the object of the Beast's persecution (e.g. Rev 5:8, 8:3, 4, 11:18, 13:7, 13:10, 14:12, 16:6, 17:6, 18:20, 24, 20:6, 9, 22:11).

5. E.g. Ryrie, *Survey*, 169, 172–73; Pentecost, *Things to Come*, 194–95.

6. See also Hultberg, *Three Views on the Rapture*; Kurschner, *Antichrist Before the Day of the Lord*; Rosenthal, *Pre-Wrath Rapture*; Van Kampen, *The Sign*.

7. A dispensation is a historical-redemptive administration during which God relates to humanity in a particular way that is different from other administrative periods (i.e. dispensations). For example, Charles C. Ryrie (*Dispensationalism Today*, 47) states, "the

major phases: classical dispensationalism (e.g. Darby, Chafer, Scofield), revised dispensationalism (e.g. Ryrie, McClain, Walvoord, Pentecost), and progressive dispensationalism (e.g. Bock, Blaising, Saucy).[8] Craig A. Blaising comments on the influence of dispensationalism from the notes of the *Scofield Reference Bible*: "The theology of the notes approached confessional status in many Bible schools, institutes, and seminaries established in the early decades of [the 20th century]."[9] He continues: "It even attained the form of a systematic theology in the work of Lewis S. Chafer [*Systematic Theology*, 8 vols (Dallas: Dallas Seminary Press, 1947)]. However, modifications were becoming evident by the 1960s, and in 1967, the notes of the *Scofield Reference Bible* were revised by an editorial committee in response to various criticisms."[10] Blaising observes,

> The new [revised] dispensationalists of the 1950s and 1960s, however, were uncomfortable with the notion of eternally separate heavenly and earthly destinies. They believed that after the Millennium, all the redeemed would be together for eternity, although they were not agreed as to where this would be. Some placed them all in "heaven"; others grouped them together on "the new earth." Consequently, the distinguishing terminology of *heavenly* and *earthly* people is scarcely found in their writings. The doctrines of the two peoples was now to be understood precisely as *Israel and the church*, a distinction

distinction between Israel and the Church . . . reflects an understanding of the basic purpose of God in all His dealings with mankind as that of glorifying Himself through salvation and other purposes as well."

8. Joseph Parle (*Dispensational Development*, 6–7) prefers the term "essentialist" to describe revised dispensationalism, because he thinks classical (Chafer) and revised (Ryrie) dispensationalism, both of which he includes as "traditional," possess minimal differences as compared to progressive dispensationalism.

9. Blaising, "Search for Definition," 21.

10. Blaising, "Search for Definition," 23.

> that Ryrie insisted must be eternally maintained, even if both were ultimately heavenly or ultimately (new) earthly people. Certain features of the earlier dispensationalism's heavenly-earthly transcendental dualism were carried over to the distinction between Israel and the church, including, for example, the parenthetical nature of the present dispensation of the church within God's national and political purpose for Israel. A remnant of the doctrine of dual destinies was retained for the Millennium [and I would add the Tribulation period]—the church inhabiting heaven, and Israel on the earth [emphasis his].[11]

While progressive dispensationalism views God working with Israel and the church at the same time, the first two phases of dispensationalism, classical and revised, which I will call "traditional dispensationalism," have maintained that, during the church age, God does *not* work with national Israel and the church simultaneously. Ryrie states: "The essence of dispensationalism, then, is the distinction between Israel and the Church."[12] Saucy, a progressive dispensationalist, further observes, "Although usually specifying the Davidic kingdom promises in particular, the fundamental teaching of traditional dispensationalism is that no part of the Old Testament kingdom predictions are being fulfilled in any way during this [church]

---

11. Blaising, "Search for Definition," 25. For a helpful history on the rise of dispensationalism, as well as its different forms and features, see Blaising and Bock, *Progressive Dispensationalism*, 9–56; Blaising, "Search for Dispensationalism," 13–34; Saucy, *Case for Progressive Dispensationalism*, 13–35; see also Parle, *Dispensational Thought*, 101–110, 123. Some posttribulationists and prewrath exponents have held to dispensationalism, or some form of it (e.g. Robert Gundry, Robert Van Kampen, Marvin Rosenthal, Charles Cooper, among others). These posttribulation and prewrath exponents, rightly, believe that the church and Israel can co-exist on earth at the same time while God works his redemptive programs respectively. Dispensational theology, then, is not an exclusive theological domain for pretribulationism.

12. Ryrie, *Dispensationalism Today*, 47.

age."[13] Revised dispensationalists eventually came to recognize, though not all are in complete agreement, that the church relates to Christ based on the Abrahamic covenant and, in some sense, the new covenant (but not the Davidic covenant).[14]

I agree that the church and national Israel should be understood as two entities. However, traditional dispensationalists have strained this distinction by claiming that God has not worked with both groups at the same time in the past, in the present, nor will he in the future during the seven-year period. Traditional dispensationalism maintains that when the church was inaugurated at Pentecost, God ceased his program with national Israel and turned exclusively to the church for the present dispensation. They hold that God will resume his redemptive program with national Israel only when Jesus returns to remove the church saints from the earth. The following traditional dispensationalists capture this fundamental premise:

Floyd Elmore:

> [Darby's secret rapture view and seventieth week theology] are really outgrowths of Darby's more basic tenet that distinguished the earthly and heavenly peoples of God. The rapture gathers the heavenly people to glory before God resumes dealings in an official way (the seventieth week) with His earthly people, the remnant of Israel.[15]

J. Dwight Pentecost:

> The present mystery [church] age intervenes within the program of God for Israel because of Israel's rejection of the Messiah at His first advent. This mystery program

---

13. Saucy, *Case for Progressive Dispensationalism*, 26–27.

14. Blaising and Bock, *Progressive Dispensationalism*, 31–46.

15. Elmore, "J. N. Darby's Early Years," 137–38, cf. Darby, *Letters*, 1:58. As noted above, later dispensational theologians dropped this untenable dichotomy of framing God's people based on "heavenly" and "earthly," while maintaining a pretribulation rapture.

> must be completed before God can resume His program with Israel and bring it to completion.[16]
>
> It must logically follow that this mystery program must itself be brought to a conclusion before God can resume His dealing with the nation Israel . . . The mystery program, which was so distinct in its inception, will certainly be separate at its conclusion. This program must be concluded before God resumes and culminates His program for Israel. *This mystery concept of the church makes a pretribulation rapture a necessity* [emphasis mine].[17]

John F. Walvoord:

> The revelation of the Church as one body requires a parenthesis between God's past dealings and His future dealings with the nation of Israel.[18]

Charles C. Ryrie:

> [E]cclesiology, or the doctrine of the church, is the touchstone of dispensationalism (and also of pretribulationism).[19]
>
> Classic dispensationalism used the words *parenthesis* or *intercalation* to describe the distinctiveness of the church in relation to God's program for Israel. An intercalation is an insertion of a period time in a calendar, and a parenthesis in one sense is defined as an interlude or interval (which in turn is defined as an intervening or interruptive period). So either or both words can be appropriately used to define the church age if one sees it as a distinct interlude in God's program for Israel (as clearly taught in Daniel's prophecy of the seventy weeks

16. Pentecost, *Things to Come*, 193, cf. 164, 247–48.

17. Pentecost, *Things to Come*, 201.

18. Walvoord, "Daniel's Seventieth Week," 48; see also Walvoord, *Rapture Question*, 2nd ed., 25.

19. Ryrie, *Dispensationalism*, 123.

> in 9:24–27) [emphasis his].[20]
>
> The distinction between Israel and the church *leads to the belief* that the church will be taken from the earth before the beginning of the Tribulation . . . Pretribulationism has become a part of normative dispensational eschatology [emphasis mine].[21]

These pretribulation statements indicate that if God's dealings with the church and Israel overlap, then their foundational presupposition is undermined. In the opening sentence of a book critiquing progressive dispensationalism, Robert L. Thomas reveals this as one of his main concerns when theologians move away from traditional dispensationalism: "[Progressive dispensationalism] differs from dispensationalism in a number of ways, one of them being not viewing the time of the rapture to be as crucial."[22] Ryrie also laments that progressive dispensationalism teaches a dispensational overlap in which God works with both Israel and the church simultaneously. Expressing his consternation, he says, "One can well ponder what will happen to the pretribulation Rapture teaching in years to come."[23] Ryrie reasoned, then, that since

20. Ryrie, *Dispensationalism*, 134.

21. Ryrie, *Dispensationalism*, 148.

22. Thomas, "Hermeneutics," 1. By "crucial," I suspect that Thomas means that if you do not hold to the traditional ecclesiastical presupposition between Israel and the church, then you do not consider the rapture question important. This, of course, is not true.

23. Ryrie, "Update," 25. See also John Brumett's "Does Progressive Dispensationalism Teach a Posttribulational Rapture?" (285–306), in which Brumett recognizes (and laments) that the distinctives of progressive dispensationalism naturally move away from a pretribulation eschatology. For example, Brumett (289) writes, "The view of one people of God appears to minimize the distinction of Israel's eschatological program with God's plan and purpose for the church which would lead to the idea that the church would be in the tribulation period and share in Daniel's seventieth week of the nation of Israel." Brumett's objection is easily answered. God at this present time is competently handling his purposes for both the church and Israel

progressive dispensationalism teaches that God works with Israel and the church simultaneously, this undermines the ecclesiastical argument for pretribulationism. *In other words, if God works with Israel and the church at the same time in this present period, then what would preclude God from working with both in the future during the seventieth week of Daniel?* Thus, Ryrie warned, "The minimizing of a clear and consistent distinction between Israel and the church results in ignoring the great prophecy of the seventy weeks in Daniel 9:24–27."[24] Ryrie was correct in his forecast of the implication for rejecting the ecclesiastical presupposition, because twenty-five years after his statement, many dispensationalists today affirm both prewrath and posttribulation views.[25]

A final point is needed. Traditional dispensationalists do not agree among themselves whether there are two new covenants, one for Israel and another for the church. Those who hold to two distinct new covenants believe that Jeremiah and Ezekiel are not referring to the same new covenant mentioned in Hebrews.[26] But many traditional dispensationalists also hold to a single new covenant in which the church in some

---

(see my main arguments below). There is diversity in unity. Brumett possesses an artificial either/or theology. See also House ("Dangers of Progressive Dispensationalism to Premillennial Theology," 329), who thinks "departure from traditional dispensationalism naturally, if not logically, results in a rejection of pretribulational premillennialism."

24. Ryrie, *Dispensationalism*, 176.

25. Cf. Cooper, "Theological Winds of Change"; idem, "Dispensational Foundations." To be sure, before progressive dispensationalism came on the scene in the late 80s, there were a few pretribulation voices who did not believe there was a necessary nor logical connection between pretribulationism and dispensational ecclesiology. They did not consider the dispensational ecclesiastical argument to be "the chief support" for pretribulationism (see especially Feinberg, "Case for the Pretribulation Rapture Position," 48–49).

26. E.g. Ryrie maintained that there were two new covenants, one for Israel and one for the church: both are "distinct and not merged into one" (*Dispensationalism*, 174); see also Chafer, *Systematic Theology*, 4:325; 7:98–99; Lewis, "The New Covenant," 135–43.

sense possesses a relationship with the new covenant of Jer 31, while it will be fulfilled in the future by Israel in the kingdom.[27]

Blaising explains the spiritualizing hermeneutic of revised dispensationalists:

> Generally, revised dispensationalists fell back on classical dispensationalism's *spiritual* hermeneutic to interpret the Old Testament's relationship to the church: the new covenant was being fulfilled *spiritually* in the church today, but Israel would experience the national and political aspects (the earthly features) of the covenant in the future. This was also the way the Abrahamic covenant was handled and the way Scofield had treated the new covenant as well. Nevertheless, they had to acknowledge a covenantal link between Israel and the church in the "literal" teaching of the New Testament [emphasis his].[28]

Dispensationalists also reconsidered their original notion of viewing the church as an absolute "parenthesis" (i.e. intercalation) within redemptive history. They began to view the church with more continuity, along with God's historical progress with Israel.[29] Further aspects of the relationship between Israel and the church were developed within dispensational theology over the next fifty years.[30] One of those key aspects, which is the focus of Part 1, is the ecclesiastical presupposition. Traditional pretribulationists argue fundamentally that since Daniel's prophecy (Dan 9:24–27) was given to Israel, the church will not be present on earth when it is fulfilled. Pretribulationists who

---

27. See Stallard, ed., *Dispensational Understanding of the New Covenant*; cf. Blaising and Bock, *Progressive Dispensationalism*, 37–38, cf. Heb 8:7–13. Blaising notes that this was argued by John F. McGahey in his doctoral dissertation at Dallas Theological Seminary in 1957 (*Progressive Dispensationalism*, 37–38).

28. Blaising and Bock, *Progressive Dispensationalism*, 38.

29. Blaising and Bock, *Progressive Dispensationalism*, 38.

30. Blaising and Bock, *Progressive Dispensationalism*, 39–56.

are *progressive* dispensational, on the other hand, are not likely to draw this conclusion since they view God working with the church and Israel simultaneously. They do not make a necessary nor logical temporal distinction because they recognize that God has, and is, working with Israel and the church simultaneously in redemptive history. For this reason, my argumentation in Part 1 is directed toward pretribulationists holding to *traditional* dispensationalism since they believe there is a necessary or theological principle between their dispensational ecclesiastical understanding of the church and Israel and pretribulationism. One exception is the traditional dispensationalist Mike Stallard, who, a pretribulationist himself, urges his fellow traditionalists not to use the church/Israel distinction as a theological proof for pretribulationism (i.e. a sufficient argument); rather, he believes it is minimally a "correlation" argument.[31] While he affirms that distinction, he believes that pretribulationism should rather be argued from exegetical arguments.[32] While I disagree with his pretribulationism, I appreciate his concern for greater precision in arguing exegetically and not based on *a priori* theological principles. I share his critique when he points out: "Covenant theology uses the covenant of grace as a theological switch by which to read the entire Bible. Progressive dispensationalism has developed enough over time that many of them are now arguing from within their system using the doctrinal conclusion of complementary hermeneutics or already-not yet as a grid by which to interpret everything in the Word."[33]

31. Stallard, "What Do Israel and the Church Share," 9–11.

32. Stallard thinks that most dispensationalists do not argue this way as a "stand-alone" argument ("What Do Israel and the Church Share," 10). While I may disagree with him on that estimate, the relevant point that I will contend in Part 1 is that the ecclesiastical presupposition is an invalid argument based on wrong premises.

33. Stallard, "What Do Israel and the Church Share," 11.

While Stallard is an exception within traditional dispensationalism, nevertheless, the critique on this point in Part 1 applies to dispensationalists who view the distinction between Israel and the church as a foundational argument for pretribulationism, or at least viewing it as a secondary or valid argument.

The theological framework of traditional dispensationalism directly shapes pretribulation theology and its interpretations of end-times passages, especially the Olivet Discourse and the book of Revelation. I agree with pretribulationism that God will fulfill his national and territorial promises to Israel when Jesus returns. Thus, I view national Israel as a distinct entity distinguished from the church. But I believe that God works out his distinct purposes for both entities simultaneously during the church age. While Israel was promised national and territorial restoration when Jesus returns, God *presently* works with Israel during the church age. At Jesus's first coming, God extended his grace to the Gentiles, while continuing to work with Israel. The ecclesiastical presupposition, however, maintains that, during the church age, God does not work with the church and Israel at the same time. Therefore, it is necessary to examine this foundational hermeneutic that controls so much of the traditional interpretive framework of pretribulationism. If it can be established that this presupposition lacks biblical support, then pretribulationism can no longer appeal to this foundational tenet.

While the critique in Part 1 will apply to traditional pretribulationists, the examination in Part 2 applies to *all* pretribulationists, regardless if they are traditional dispensationalists, progressive dispensationalists, or non-dispensationalists, because all pretribulationists disconnect the rapture from the second coming by placing a seven-year gap between them.

Conclusion

In this chapter, I situated the theology of dispensationalism by providing a sketch of its history and distinctives. I focused on pretribulationists who hold to the traditional dispensational framework and maintain an absolute, sharp, and temporal distinction between God's programs for Israel and the church. Traditional pretribulationists infer from their ecclesiastical framework that the rapture of the church must happen before God "resumes" his program with Israel for the final seventieth week of Daniel. In the next chapter, I will examine this misunderstanding of Daniel's prophecy. For traditional dispensational pretribulationism, Dan 9:24–27 is their most frequently cited proof text.

Chapter 2

'SEVENTY WEEKS HAVE BEEN DECREED FOR YOUR PEOPLE'

In the last chapter, I outlined dispensational theology, explaining that traditional dispensationalism places a temporal separation between national Israel and the church, where God focuses on one program at a time in history. Traditional dispensationalists reason, then, that the rapture of the church must happen before God reinstitutes his program with Israel during the seventieth week of Daniel. In this chapter, I will focus on the "seventy weeks" prophecy and the pretribulation claim that it precludes the church from being present on earth during that time.

The seventy weeks prophecy is the main proof text used by traditional dispensationalists for the ecclesiastical presupposition:

> Seventy weeks have been determined concerning your people and your holy city to put an end to rebellion, to bring sin to completion, to atone for iniquity, to bring in perpetual righteousness, to seal up the prophetic vision, and to anoint a most holy place. So know and understand: From the issuing of the command to restore and rebuild Jerusalem until an anointed one, a prince arrives, there

> will be a period of seven weeks and sixty-two weeks. It will again be built, with plaza and moat, but in distressful times. Now after the sixty-two weeks, an anointed one will be cut off and have nothing. As for the city and the sanctuary, the people of the coming prince will destroy them. But his end will come speedily like a flood. Until the end of the war that has been decreed there will be destruction. He will confirm a covenant with many for one week. But in the middle of that week he will bring sacrifices and offerings to a halt. On the wing of abominations will come one who destroys, until the decreed end is poured out on the one who destroys (Dan 9:24–27).

The prophet Daniel anguished over the sins of rebellious Israel, praying to God by confessing on behalf of his nation and asking for mercy, forgiveness, and repentance. While Daniel was praying, God sent a prophetic word through the angel Gabriel. Daniel was told that God would decree a block of time of 490 years to complete Israel's captivity: "Seventy weeks [i.e. 490 years] have been determined concerning your people and your holy city to put an end to rebellion, to bring sin to completion, to atone for iniquity, to bring in perpetual righteousness, to seal up the prophetic vision, and to anoint a most holy place" (Dan 9:24). The decree of Artaxerxes in 444 BC to Nehemiah to rebuild Jerusalem and its walls most likely initiated Daniel's prophecy (Neh 2:1–8).[1] The first sixty-nine weeks of Daniel's prophecy have already been fulfilled (i.e. 483 years, cf. Dan 9:25–26).[2] Futurists, such as myself, believe the last seven

1. See Tanner, *Daniel*, 569–87. Summarizing his extensive argumentation, Tanner (*Daniel*, 582) outlines: "(1) Nehemiah's request to Artaxerxes was specifically to rebuild the city (Neh 2:5–8); (2) the book of Nehemiah (and Ezra 4:7–23) indicates that the restoration was done in the most distressing circumstances (note the ending to Dan 9:25!); and (3) this is the only view, if the numbers are to be taken literally, that harmonizes with an AD 33 date for Christ's crucifixion . . . ."

2. See Hoehner, *Chronological Aspects*, 115–39.

years remain to be fulfilled, completing Daniel's 490-year prophecy when national Israel's salvation is accomplished. Since the vast majority of the readers of this book will assume a futurist framework of prophecy, it is not necessary to take the time to defend the futurity of the seven-year period.[3] But I want to make a couple of comments on this temporal framework. An important verse in this passage is Dan 9:27:

> He [a Beast figure] will confirm a covenant with many [Israel] for one week [i.e. seven years]. But in the middle of that week he will bring sacrifices and offerings to a halt. On the wing of abominations will come one who destroys, until the decreed end is poured out on the one who destroys.[4]

This verse states that "he" will confirm a covenant with many for "one week" (*šābûa*), which in this Hebrew context denotes seven years. The New English Translation renders the Hebrew verb *gābar* as "confirm." The English Standard Version renders it "make a strong covenant." But the sense behind the Hebrew may better indicate enforcing, imposing, or coercing, suggesting that the other party to the covenant may not have much say in the matter (HALOT).[5] The Beast will cause an abomination by breaking the covenant and stopping the sacrifices and offerings. This will occur in the middle of Daniel's seventieth week (i.e. the midpoint of the seven-year period). Accordingly, the "many" likely refers to Israel, or more specifically, the Jewish religious leadership, since the covenant relates to the stopping of the sacrifices

---

3. For a full-orbed, exegetical treatment of Daniel's prophecy, see Tanner, *Daniel*, 543–615.

4. Cf. Dan 12:11: "From the time that the daily sacrifice is removed and the abomination that causes desolation is set in place, there are 1,290 days."

5. Tanner suggests, considering the "sacrifice and offering" context, this could indicate that the antichrist will be a false messiah duping Israel and causing the Mosaic covenant to be the law of the land (*Daniel*, 592–96).

and offerings associated with the Jewish temple.

Having outlined Daniel's seventy-weeks prophecy, we turn to the pretribulation interpretation of this prophecy. Traditional pretribulation interpreters argue that the church cannot be present on earth during any part of the seventieth week because that is when God resumes his dealings with Israel. They argue that since the church did not exist during the first sixty-nine weeks (i.e. 483 years), it therefore will not be present on earth during the seventieth week (i.e. seven years). Pentecost represents the traditional pretribulation view:

> Since [the church] had no part in the first sixty-nine weeks, which are related only to God's program for Israel, it can have no part in the seventieth week, which is again related to God's program for Israel after the mystery program for the church has been concluded.[6]

Michael A. Rydelnik shares this point with traditional dispensationalism based on *a priori* reasoning:

> The distinction between the church and Israel should yield a belief that the rapture of the church will take place before the tribulation of the end of days (a pretribulation rapture) [. . . .] The Seventieth Week (the tribulation period) begins when God turns His primary attention once again to Israel after the removal of the church. This entire prophecy pertains to Israel and not to the church at all.[7]

Charles C. Ryrie gives this as a main reason he holds to pretribulationism:

> If the church had no part in the first sixty-nine weeks of Daniel's prophecy, how can it be a part of the future seventieth week?[8]

---

6. Pentecost, *Things to Come*, 196.

7. Rydelnik, "Israel," 256–57; cf. Patterson, "Israel and the Great Tribulation," 70.

8. Ryrie, *Premillennial Faith*, 144.

Similarly, Walvoord articulates a version of this argument:

> Israel's [seventy weeks] program is therefore at a standstill [at this time] . . . .[9]

He further states:

> The unity of Daniel's seventieth week is maintained by pretribulationists. By contrast, [other views] destroy the unity of Daniel's seventieth week and confuse Israel's program with that of the church.[10]

In summary, then, traditional pretribulationism reasons that the church will not be part of the seventieth week of Daniel because it was not part of the sixty-nine weeks. This understanding is problematic for several reasons.

It is logically flawed to argue that since the church did not exist during the first sixty-nine weeks, it is precluded from existing during the seventieth week. The church had not yet been formed during the sixty-nine weeks. However, the relevant fact is that *the church exists now*. Its existence does not, in itself, preclude it from being here when the seventieth week begins, co-existing with Israel as God works with both.

A lexical fallacious version has been heard on occasion, which claims that since Daniel's prophecy, and his seventieth week, does not mention the word *church*, this is evidence that the church will not exist during the seventieth week.[11] We can illustrate this flawed lexical, word-concept fallacy with the following example. There is no mention of the word "church" in the vision of the metal statue in Daniel 2 representing the major kingdoms, which includes imperial Rome. Using pretribulation reasoning, it must follow that the church could not have existed on earth during the Roman

---

9. Walvoord, *Rapture Question*, 2nd ed., 126.

10. Walvoord, *Rapture Question*, 2nd ed., 271, cf. Feinberg, "Arguing about the Rapture," 196–97.

11. E.g. Hoyt, *The End Times*, 137.

period either![12] Moreover, there are two parts of Daniel's seventy weeks prophecy that cover the church period. First, Daniel's prophecy indicates a gap of time between the period of sixty-two weeks (Dan 9:25–26) and the seventieth week (Dan 9:27). Even though the "church" is not mentioned, every pretribulationist would agree that the church exists during this time. Moreover, Daniel's prophecy predicted the destruction of Jerusalem and the temple by the Romans, *which occurred in AD 70 during the church age* ("As for the city and the sanctuary, the people of the coming prince will destroy them" (Dan 9:26).

Even though pretribulation interpreter Renald E. Showers agrees that God works with both the church and Israel during the gap between the sixty-ninth week and the seventieth week, he believes that God will not work with the church during Daniel's seventieth week. Showers makes the following theological-interpretive move by excluding the church from existing on earth during any of the seventieth week of Daniel:

> The church did not exist during any part of the first 69 weeks or 483 years of the 70 weeks. . . . [which is consistent with the view] that God determined all 70 weeks specifically for Israel and Jerusalem, not for the church.[13]

He further reiterates his imposition of the theological-ecclesiastical hermeneutic:

> God does not intend the church to be present on the earth for any part of the 70 weeks or 490 years He has determined specifically for Israel and Jerusalem. He intends to keep His 70-weeks program for Israel and Jerusalem and His program for the church separate and distinct from each other, just as Israel and the church are distinct entities.[14]

12. This point was shared with me by Greg Anderson in personal correspondence.

13. Showers, *Maranatha*, 241.

14. Showers, *Maranatha*, 243. By "separate," he means that they

He then makes the following interpretive move:

> This does not mean that God stopped working altogether with Israel and Jerusalem when He interrupted the 70-weeks program and started the church. Instead, it means that God temporarily stopped one specific program (the 70-weeks program) with Israel and Jerusalem while He works His program with the church in the world. There is a major difference between saying that God stopped working with Israel *altogether* and saying that He temporarily stopped *one specific program* with that nation [emphasis mine].[15]

Showers' view is flawed and lacks exegetical support. He rightly recognizes that God works with both Israel and the church *between* the sixty-ninth and seventieth week. However, he fails to explain exegetically why the church is excluded from God's dealings during the seventieth week. Merely asserting that God made the prophecy to Israel is not an argument for the church's exclusion. It brings me back to my point that it does not logically follow that the church must be excluded from the seventieth week simply because it did not exist during the first sixty-nine. Showers asserts his position rather than defends it. His argument does not go to the extreme by claiming that God does not work with both Israel and the church in the present church age, but it is invalid to object that God will not work with the church and Israel during the seventieth week of Daniel.[16]

---

will not exist on earth simultaneously during any of the seventy-weeks prophecy. This is a huge theological imposition.

15. Showers, *Maranatha*, 243.

16. Incidentally, it should be noted that the seventy weeks prophecy is not completely unrelated to the gap period. Both the seventy-weeks prophecy and the gap include the purpose of judgment for Israel. God judges Israel both during the seventy weeks prophecy using Gentile nations and during the period between the sixty-ninth and seventieth weeks. Thus, while there is a gap between the sixty-ninth and seventieth week, there is similarity in the program of God's purposes.

More to the main point, Daniel's passage is specifically addressing Israel ("concerning your people and your holy city"). It also relates to unbelieving Gentiles because it identifies who will be oppressing Israel during this time. Daniel's prophecy is not making claims for *excluding* the future church. That makes Daniel's prophecy say more than it does. The assumption that the church will be excluded from the last seven years is being read into the prophecy. Daniel's prophecy is a positive statement *for* Israel, not a negative statement *about* the church. Further, there is a glaring inconsistency that pretribulation interpreters fail to recognize. While they maintain "a worldwide revival" of Gentiles during Daniel's seventieth week, Daniel's prophecy in Dan 9:24–27 is *completely silent on that so-called event.* Pretribulationists cannot claim the church is absent because it is not mentioned in the prophecy while claiming that a worldwide revival of Gentiles will take place! To be sure, they argue that the Bible depicts a revival of "tribulation saints," but this is not found in Dan 9. They construe this from the New Testament in Rev 7 as a "revival."[17] Robert H. Gundry rightly notes, "So progress in the biblical history of salvation makes the situation in a future seventieth week different from what it was during the past sixty-nine weeks. You can't legitimately argue from one to the other."[18] Broadening our Old Testament scope, then, from Dan 9:24–27, Gundry points out a similar inconsistency:

> Both [pretribs and non-pretribs] agree that a large number

17. For example, John MacArthur (*Revelation 1–11*, 222, cf. 223–25), commenting on Rev 7:9–17, writes, "[T]here is coming in the future a worldwide response to the gospel that will far exceed any other in history and maybe all others combined. It will sweep the globe in just a few short years and produce a vast multitude of redeemed people from all the nations, making it the greatest movement of God's saving power the world will ever see" (cf. Walvoord, *Revelation*, 144; Ryrie, *Revelation*, 74–75).

18. Gundry, *First the Antichrist*, 135.

> of Gentile saints [. . .] will live on earth during the tribulation (so, clearly, Rev. 7:9–17). But do any tribulational passages in the OT mention those Gentile saints? No such passages are adduced. If none exist, pretribulationists should hardly argue from a mysterious silence in the OT concerning the Church, because the OT remains silent also concerning the Gentile saints whom we know to be on earth during the tribulation.[19]

Through progressive revelation, the New Testament reveals the overlay of the church during Daniel's final seven-year prophecy in which God works with Israel and the church simultaneously to accomplish his purposes. God's revelation of Daniel's prophecy is *augmented* with more events from the New Testament, just as Old Testament prophecies are augmented with more events from the New Testament; e.g. the identity of the Messiah and details of his life and ministry.

As a final note, pretribulation theology typically calls Daniel's seventieth week a "Jewish week." But more accurately, it should be called a "Gentile week" because Daniel's prophecy establishes *all* seventy weeks (including the last week of seven years) dominated by unbelieving *Gentiles*. Only after the completion of the entire block of 490 years of Gentile domination will Daniel's prophecy of Israel's restoration be fulfilled, not before.[20]

---

19. Gundry, *Church and the Tribulation*, 12–13.

20. Some traditional dispensationalists (e.g. Chafer, *Major Bible Themes*, 100) have understood the seventieth week as an extension of the period of the Mosaic Law with the reconstitution of its legal principles: e.g. God ordained Sabbath, sacrifices, etc. It is believed that since the sixty-nine weeks occurred during the dispensation of the Law, then it follows that the seventieth week will be a reconstitution of the Mosaic Law. Ryrie, a traditional dispensationalist himself, disagreed with some of his fellow dispensationalists who believed that the reconstitution of the Mosaic Law will occur during the seventieth week: "The principal objection to this view is simply that no other dispensation comes back into effect again once it has ended, and there is no question that the Mosaic Law ended with the first advent

Conclusion

In this chapter, I explained why the pretribulation ecclesiastical presupposition based on Daniel's prophecy is predicated on flawed assumptions. The purpose of Daniel's prophecy is to answer the question when national Israel will come to repentance. It was not intended to address whether the church would be present or absent during the seventieth week. In the next chapter, I will follow several lines of evidence that demonstrate that God has worked simultaneously with both national Israel and the church in the past, does so in the present, and will continue to do so in the future, including during Daniel's seventieth week.

---

of Christ (Rom. 10:4, 2 Cor. 3:7–11)" (Ryrie, *Dispensationalism*, 50). In addition, Ryrie, who held to seven dispensations, refuted other traditional dispensationalists who construed "The Tribulation" (i.e. the seventieth week) as a separate, distinguishable dispensation in itself, resulting, then, in eight dispensations within their theological system. He responded by giving good reasons for the continuity between the church age and the seventieth week, thereby militating against the understanding that the seventieth week will be a new, distinguishable dispensation: e.g. observance of the Sabbath by unbelieving Jews in the present church age and during the seventieth week, and Gentiles and Jews coming to know Jesus through the preaching of the gospel of the cross in this present church age and during the seventieth week. Finally, since the sixty-nine weeks are never considered a separate, distinguishable dispensation, there is no good reason to consider the seventieth week as one (Ryrie, *Dispensationalism*, 50–51). Ryrie holds that the seventieth week completes the final period of the dispensation of grace, since it is characterized mostly by God's judgments upon those who have rejected the gospel and expressions of Jewish and Gentile saints believing in Christ (Ryrie, *Dispensationalism*, 50–57).

Chapter 3

GOD WORKS WITH ISRAEL AND THE CHURCH SIMULTANEOUSLY

In the last chapter, I critiqued the pretribulation understanding of Dan 9:24–27 that the church will be excluded from the seventieth week of Daniel when God "resumes" his program with Israel. In this chapter, I will continue to respond to the ecclesiastical presupposition that God does not work with Israel and the church at the same time. I will consider evidence that God has worked with both Israel and the church simultaneously in the past, does in the present, and will do so during the seventieth week. This chapter is a critique of traditional dispensationalism, which operates from the ecclesiastical presupposition that creates a sharp temporal separation between Israel and the church. For pretribulation proponents who hold to progressive dispensationalism or a non-dispensational framework, this chapter may not apply to them. To be sure, they may believe that God only works with Israel during the seventieth week but may do so on different grounds, particularly based on the Parousia presupposition, which will be the focus in Part 2.[1]

1. E.g. Blaising, "Case for the Pretribulation Rapture," 68–72. Blaising ("Case

God Has Worked with Israel and the Church Simultaneously in the Past

There are key Old Testament messianic prophecies given to Israel that were fulfilled during the establishment of the church in the first century. As such the interpreter should not find it surprising that God will work with both Israel and the church in the future during the seven-year period. In this section, I will identify three Old Covenant prophecies given to Israel—and about Israel—that began to be fulfilled during the establishment of the church. The point is to show that because God has worked with both Israel and the church simultaneously in the past, there is no necessary theological inference to exclude the church from existing on earth in the future during the seventieth week.

The New Covenant (Jer 31:31–34)

The first prophecy I will examine is the new covenant prophecy promised in the Old Testament by the prophet Jeremiah:

> "Indeed, a time is coming," says the LORD, "when I will make a new covenant with the people of Israel and Judah. It will not be like the old covenant that I made with their ancestors when I delivered them from Egypt. For they violated that covenant, even though I was like a faithful husband to them," says the LORD. "But I will make a new covenant with the whole nation of Israel after I plant them back in the land," says the LORD. "I will put my law within

---

for the Pretribulation Rapture," 71) writes, "For progressive dispensationalists, the rapture occurs at the beginning of the tribulation because God wills it so, as revealed by Paul in his Thessalonian correspondence, not because it is necessary to separate the program of the church." He further notes, "A pretribulational rapture rests upon its logical relationship to the onset of the day of the Lord . . . . Consequently, I find the ecclesial status [i.e. the ecclesiastical presupposition] of these tribulation believers to be irrelevant to the timing of the rapture" (Blaising, "A Pretribulation Response," 156, cf. 155–56).

> them and write it on their hearts and minds. I will be their God and they will be my people. People will no longer need to teach their neighbors and relatives to know me. For all of them, from the least important to the most important, will know me," says the LORD. "For I will forgive their sin and will no longer call to mind the wrong they have done" (Jer 31:31–34).

This passage states that God promised to make a new covenant with "the people of Israel and Judah." It was not promised to the church. However, in the New Testament we learn that certain benefits have been extended to Gentiles, even though they are not part of Israel. The church is governed under the Jewish new covenant.[2] If a traditional pretribulationist were consistent with this hermeneutic, they would need to insist that the church cannot exist on earth during the new covenant, since it was promised to Israel (and as noted earlier, some traditional dispensationalists believe in two new covenants). Pretribulationists possess one interpretative standard for Daniel's prophecy and another for Jeremiah's new covenant prophecy. To put it another way, they take the fuller New Testament revelation into consideration for the new covenant prophecy, applying it to both Israel and the church, but they do not take the fuller New Testament revelation for Daniel's prophecy and do the same. It is invalid to claim that because Daniel's prophecy was made to Israel, and about Israel, it must exclude the church from the final seven-year period. Jeremiah's prophecy to Israel, therefore, renders this pretribulation hermeneutic flawed. I'll conclude my point on this prophecy with George

2. While the church does not appear in this Old Testament prophecy, Jeremiah's prophecy relates to the new covenant described in the New Testament, which demonstrates that the benefits of this covenant extend to the Gentiles (1 Cor 11:25, 2 Cor 3:6, Heb 7:22, 8:6, 8:8–12, 9:15, 10:16, 12:24, 13:20–21, Gal 4:21–31, Rom 11:16–29, Eph 2:11–22).

Eldon Ladd, who captures this point:

> If then we have the principle clearly established that prophecies which in the Old Testament have to do with God's future purpose for Israel have their fulfillment both in the Church and in Israel, why should we not conclude that the prophecies about the Great Tribulation which have to do in their prophetic form with Israel will find their fulfillment both in the Church and in Israel, unless the Word of God clearly asserts the contrary? We are on church ground, not Jewish ground in Acts 2 and Hebrews 8 even though the Old Testament predictions appear to be exclusively on Jewish ground. Why are we not also on church ground as well as on Jewish ground in Matthew 24 and Revelation 13? The assumption that this is exclusively Jewish ground is a human interpretation which is not supported by the Word of God.[3]

Pouring Out of the Spirit (Joel 2:28–31)

In Ladd's statement above, he alluded to Acts, which mentions a second prophecy from the Old Testament in the book of Joel:

> After all of this I will pour out my Spirit on all kinds of people. Your sons and daughters will prophesy. Your elderly will have revelatory dreams; your young men will see prophetic visions. Even on male and female servants I will pour out my Spirit in those days. I will produce portents both in the sky and on the earth—blood, fire, and columns of smoke. The sunlight will be turned to darkness and the moon to the color of blood, *before* the day of the LORD comes—that great and terrible day! (Joel 2:28–31).

This prophecy began to be fulfilled in the context of Israel *and* the establishment of the church age. Preaching at Pentecost, Peter proclaims:

---

3. Ladd, *Blessed Hope*, 133.

> "But this is what was spoken about through the prophet Joel: 'And in the last days it will be,' God says, 'that I will pour out my Spirit on all people, and your sons and your daughters will prophesy, and your young men will see visions, and your old men will dream dreams. Even on my servants, both men and women, I will pour out my Spirit in those days, and they will prophesy. And I will perform wonders in the sky above and miraculous signs on the earth below, blood and fire and clouds of smoke. The sun will be changed to darkness and the moon to blood before the great and glorious day of the Lord comes. And then everyone who calls on the name of the Lord will be saved'" (Acts 2:16–21).

Peter takes the Old Testament prophecy from the prophet Joel, which was originally given to Israel, and extends it to the church. Joel's prophecy to Israel then began to be fulfilled during the time of Israel *and* during the new spiritual community composed of Jews and Gentiles—i.e. the church.[4] It should be clarified that, while these events were prophesied originally to Israel, the church is not "replacing" Israel. Instead, the application of the prophecy is being extended to the believing Gentiles in the church through the coming of the Holy Spirit. The implication is clear: Since the church age was *established* during the fulfillment of a Jewish prophecy, in principle, then, the church age can be *completed* during the fulfillment of the Jewish prophecy of Daniel's seventieth week.

Peter does not view Joel's entire prophecy as being completely fulfilled at Pentecost. Peter construes Joel's prophecy as having begun to be fulfilled. In other words, Peter's understanding of Joel's prophecy is likened to

4. Incidentally, an argument can be made that church truth began to be preached earlier, or at least overlapped with the Mosaic dispensation during Jesus's ministry (cf. Luke 5:33–39, 16:16, Matt 9:14–17, 11:13, Mark 2:21–22, 7:18–19, John 1:17, Heb 2:3, 1 Tim 6:3).

bookends to the church age. The first part occurred during the pouring out of the Spirit on all people, which revealed that God was doing a new redemptive work. At that time, the church age was *conceived*. The second part of Joel's prophecy concerns the celestial disturbances announcing the day of the Lord's judgment, which remains to be fulfilled. At that future time, the church age will be *completed* (see also Luke 21:25–28, Matt 24:22–31, Mark 13:20–27, Rev 6:12–8:5, Joel 2:31). Therefore, since the establishment of the church is involved in the fulfillment of an Old Testament prophecy given to Israel, it cannot be maintained that the church cannot be involved during the prophecy of Daniel's seventy weeks, a prophecy that was also given to Israel. In short, God has worked with Israel and the church simultaneously. As Gundry puts it, "since the beginning of the Church age bears a marked relationship to OT predictions concerning Israel, we are not hindered dispensationally from presuming that the same will be so at the end of the Church age."[5]

God Judged Israel in AD 70 (Matt 24:1–2, Luke 19:43–44)

The next Old Testament prophecy is Jesus's prediction of the judgment on Israel. During the Old Covenant dispensation, Jesus prophesied to Israel that God would judge Jerusalem with destruction, including its temple:

> Now as Jesus was going out of the temple courts and walking away, his disciples came to show him the temple buildings. And he said to them, "Do you see all these things? I tell you the truth, not one stone will be left on another. All will be torn down!" (Matt 24:1–2, cf. Luke 21:5–6).

> "For the days will come upon you when your enemies will build an embankment against you and surround you and

---

5. Gundry, *Church and the Tribulation*, 15.

> close in on you from every side. They will demolish you—you and your children within your walls—and they will not leave within you one stone on top of another, because you did not recognize the time of your visitation from God" (Luke 19:43–44).

When did this prophecy *to* Israel *concerning* Israel become fulfilled? It took place in AD 70—during the *church age*.

In summary, these three biblical examples illustrate that God has worked with Israel and the church simultaneously: (1) Jeremiah prophesied to Israel about the promise of the new covenant that God would make with Israel, benefits that have been not replaced by, but extended to the church. (2) Joel made a prophecy originally given to Israel and fulfilled in the context of both Israel and the church, at Pentecost. (3) Jesus made a prophecy to Israel, and about Israel, concerning its judgment, which was fulfilled in AD 70 during the church age. These three Old Testament prophecies invalidate the ecclesiastical presupposition of traditional pretribulationism that the church must be removed from the earth before Daniel's seventieth week. These Old Testament prophecies were prophesied to Israel and had fulfillments in the church age. There is no necessary, theological principle or hermeneutic that would prevent the church from being on earth when the seventieth week begins.

God Works with Israel and the Church Simultaneously in the Present

God continues to work his redemptive program with Israel at this present time *during the church age*. In this section, I will consider two significant divine activities currently related to Israel. First, God is making Israel jealous and saving a Jewish remnant; second, God is regathering Israel to a homeland.

Making Israel Jealous and Saving a Remnant

In Rom 9–11, the apostle Paul articulates his faith that God has not nullified his promises for national Israel. Instead, he will keep them, despite Israel's present unbelief. In this section, I will highlight God's *present* activity with Israel that will culminate in their salvation at the completion of Daniel's seventieth week. Paul cites the prophecy about God making Israel jealous by extending his salvation to the Gentiles:

> But again I ask, didn't Israel understand? First Moses says, "I will make you jealous by those who are not a nation; with a senseless nation I will provoke you to anger." And Isaiah is even bold enough to say, "I was found by those who did not seek me; I became well known to those who did not ask for me" (Rom 10:19–20, cf. 10:21—11:10).

In this passage, Paul cites two Old Covenant prophets, Moses and Isaiah, concerning their prophecies that grace would be found by others (i.e. Gentiles). Paul responds to Moses's and Isaiah's prophecies exclaiming God's faithfulness to his promise to Israel:

> I ask then, they did not stumble into an irrevocable fall, did they? Absolutely not! But by their transgression salvation has come to the Gentiles, to make Israel jealous. Now if their transgression means riches for the world and their defeat means riches for the Gentiles, how much more will their full restoration bring? Now I am speaking to you Gentiles. Seeing that I am an apostle to the Gentiles, I magnify my ministry, if somehow I could provoke my people to jealousy and save some of them. For if their rejection is the reconciliation of the world, what will their acceptance be but life from the dead? . . . For I do not want you to be ignorant of this mystery, brothers and sisters, so that you may not be conceited: A partial hardening has happened to Israel until the full number of the Gentiles has come in (Rom 11:11–15, 25).

God is using the salvation of Gentiles as a means of

provoking Israel to come to salvation, saving a remnant at the present time. God is *not inactive* with Israel. He has not "postponed" his dealings with Israel. Rather, he is actively making them jealous by extending his grace to the Gentiles. While he extends his grace to Gentiles, he is saving—now, in the present—a Jewish remnant, for "a *partial* hardening has happened to Israel." This partial hardening will be removed when "the full number of the Gentiles has come in" (Rom 11:25). At that time, "all Israel will be saved" (Rom 11:26). Through the centuries, God has been working with Israel by enlightening Jews daily by the power of the Gospel. Paul, therefore, taught that God works at this time through both hardening and enlightening Israel.

In addition, while God continues to work with national Israel, the Old Testament prophet Isaiah prophesied that Israel would be a witness to the Gentiles: "Is it too insignificant a task for you to be my servant, to reestablish the tribes of Jacob, and restore the remnant of Israel? I will make you a light to the nations, so you can bring my deliverance to the remote regions of the earth" (Isa 49:6). Some may object that this prophecy is instead speaking of the millennium. That objection does not work because in the book of Acts, Paul and Barnabas refer to this prophecy as a contemporaneous fulfillment, a command from the Lord to evangelize Gentiles *in this age*: "For this is what the Lord has commanded us: 'I have appointed you to be a light for the Gentiles, to bring salvation to the ends of the earth'" (Acts 13:47, cf. 26:23). In summary, these points demonstrate that God currently works with Israel and the church simultaneously.[6]

6. Peter notes that the Old Testament prophets write about this prophesied grace: "Concerning this salvation, the prophets who predicted the grace that would come to you searched and investigated carefully. They probed into what person or time the Spirit of Christ within them was indicating when he testified beforehand about the sufferings appointed for Christ and his subsequent glory. They were shown that they were serving not themselves but you, in regard to

Regathering Israel to a Homeland

Another divine program with Israel during the current church age is God regathering Israel back to her homeland. In the late 1800s, a trickling of Jews began to take place in such a regathering.[7] Eventually, in 1948, in the aftermath of World War 2, Israel once again became a nation in her homeland. Today, God continues to providentially regather Jews around the world, even saving many of them. This contradicts the ecclesiastical presupposition that understands God as not dealing with national Israel during the church age and only resuming his program with Israel in the future when the seventieth week begins. God's regathering program is attested by Ezekiel's "dry bones" prophecy in Ezek 37:1–14:

> The hand of the LORD was on me, and he brought me out by the Spirit of the LORD and placed me in the midst of the valley, and it was full of bones. He made me walk all around among them. I realized there were a great many bones in the valley and they were very dry. He said to me, "Son of man, can these bones live?" I said to him, "Sovereign Lord, you know." Then he said to me, "Prophesy over these bones, and tell them: 'Dry bones, hear the word of the LORD. This is what the sovereign LORD says to these bones: Look, I am about to infuse breath into you and you will live. I will put tendons on you and muscles over you and will cover you with skin; I will put breath in you and you will live. Then you will know that I am the LORD.'"
>
> So I prophesied as I was commanded. There was a sound when I prophesied—I heard a rattling, and the bones came together, bone to bone. As I watched, I saw tendons on

the things now announced to you through those who proclaimed the gospel to you by the Holy Spirit sent from heaven—things angels long to catch a glimpse of. Therefore, get your minds ready for action by being fully sober, and set your hope completely on the grace that will be brought to you when Jesus Christ is revealed" (1 Pet 1:10–13).

7. Morris, *1948*, 2–21.

> them, then muscles appeared, and skin covered over them from above, but there was no breath in them.
>
> He said to me, "Prophesy to the breath—prophesy, son of man—and say to the breath: 'This is what the sovereign LORD says: Come from the four winds, O breath, and breathe on these corpses so that they may live.'" So I prophesied as I was commanded, and the breath came into them; they lived and stood on their feet, an extremely great army.
>
> Then he said to me, "Son of man, these bones are all the house of Israel. Look, they are saying, 'Our bones are dry, our hope has LORD; we are cut off.' Therefore prophesy, and tell them, 'This is what the sovereign LORD says: Look, I am about to open your graves and will raise you from your graves, my people. I will bring you to the land of Israel. Then you will know that I am the LORD, when I open your graves and raise you from your graves, my people. I will place my breath in you and you will live; I will give you rest in your own land. Then you will know that I am the LORD—I have spoken and I will act, declares the LORD.'"

In his prophecy, Ezekiel uses biological metaphors to indicate three phases to Israel's salvation ("Son of man, *these bones are all the house of Israel*"). In the first phase, her exiled circumstances are represented as "dry bones," "corpses," and "our bones are dry, our hope has perished; *we are cut off.*" The second phase is Israel's present regathering to her homeland, but in an unregenerate, unbelieving status, rejecting Jesus as her messiah. But this phase includes a believing remnant, which is realized as "a rattling, and the bones came together, bone to bone. As I watched, I saw tendons on them, then muscles appeared, and skin covered over them from above, *but there was no breath in them.*" Ezekiel also indicates this regathering, saying, "I will bring you to the land of Israel." The third and final phase is Israel's salvation, which is signaled by the key term *breath*: "I will place my breath in you and you will live; I will give you rest in your own land. Then you will know that I am the LORD."

The prophet Ezekiel made a prophecy to Israel, and about Israel, with much of it being fulfilled during the church age. God's regathering of Israel did not wait until the seventieth week of Daniel to begin. God has already initiated those aspects of his program to regather them to their homeland. The ecclesiastical presupposition is invalidated by Ezekiel's prophecy.

God Will Work with Israel and the Church Simultaneously in the Future

We have established a biblical pattern of God working with both Israel and the church simultaneously in the past and the present. If God is working with both Israel and the church in the present age, it should not be surprising that Scripture affirms that God will work with both simultaneously in the future, too, particularly during much of the seven-year period.

A juxtaposition occurs in Rev 7 where God protects two groups before the opening of the seventh seal. The first group is the 144,000 "from all the tribes of the people of Israel."

> After this I saw four angels standing at the four corners of the earth, holding back the four winds of the earth so no wind could blow on the earth, on the sea, or on any tree. Then I saw another angel ascending from the east, who had the seal of the living God. He shouted out with a loud voice to the four angels who had been given permission to damage the earth and the sea: "Do not damage the earth or the sea or the trees until we have put a seal on the foreheads of the servants of our God." Now I heard the number of those who were marked with the seal, one hundred and forty-four thousand, sealed from all the tribes of the

> people of Israel: From the tribe of Judah, twelve thousand were sealed, from the tribe of Reuben, twelve thousand, from the tribe of Gad, twelve thousand, from the tribe of Asher, twelve thousand, from the tribe of Naphtali, twelve thousand, from the tribe of Manasseh, twelve thousand, from the tribe of Simeon, twelve thousand, from the tribe of Levi, twelve thousand, from the tribe of Issachar, twelve thousand, from the tribe of Zebulun, twelve thousand, from the tribe of Joseph, twelve thousand, from the tribe of Benjamin, twelve thousand were sealed (Rev 7:1–8).

These 144,000, at least in part, are the remnant of national Israel who will convert at the end of the seventieth week, thereby fulfilling the prophecy in Dan 9:24–27.[8] God will spiritually save them when they recognize Jesus as their long-awaited messiah (cf. Rev 14:1–5, Zech 12:10). They are protected on earth during God's wrath because they have the "seal" placed on their foreheads: "Do not damage the earth or the sea or the trees until we have put a seal on the foreheads of the servants of our God" (Rev 7:3).

Another group, simultaneously, is protected from the impending eschatological wrath of God. This group, however, is not protected on earth but delivered to heaven,

8. I do not view the 144,000 Israelites in Rev 7:4–8 as saved at the moment they are sealed. Rather, I view the sealing in the sense of God choosing this group to *become saved* when they recognize Jesus as Messiah at the completion of the seven-year period, fulfilling Daniel's prophecy of Israel's salvation. They are sealed at this point for physical protection from the impending wrath of God via the trumpet and bowl judgments (cf. Rev 9:4). Some may object that the 144,000 are saved at the moment they are sealed because they are described as "bond-servants." However, as Robert Gundry (*Church and the Tribulation*, 82) has pointed out, this is not a necessary conclusion: "The designation 'bond-servants' (7:3), then, anticipates their role in the reestablishment of the Davidic kingdom. Isaiah calls unregenerate Israel the 'servant' of the Lord (42:18–25) in *anticipation* of the nation's restoration (43:1ff.)—exactly the interpretation here given for the 144,000 [see also similar anticipatory statements in, for example, Jer 1:5, Luke 1:15] (emphasis mine)."

ushered before the throne of God.[9] They are described as an innumerable crowd who appear in heaven "having come out of the great tribulation."

> After these things I looked, and here was an enormous crowd that no one could count, made up of persons from every nation, tribe, people, and language, standing before the throne and before the Lamb dressed in long white robes, and with palm branches in their hands. They were shouting out in a loud voice, "Salvation belongs to our God, to the one seated on the throne, and to the Lamb!" And all the angels stood there in a circle around the throne and around the elders and the four living creatures, and they threw themselves down with their faces to the ground before the throne and worshiped God, saying, "Amen! Praise and glory, and wisdom and thanksgiving, and honor and power and strength be to our God for ever and ever. Amen!" Then one of the elders asked me, "These dressed in long white robes—who are they and where have they come from?" So I said to him, "My lord, you know the answer." Then he said to me, "These are the ones who have come out of the great tribulation. They have washed their robes and made them white in the blood of the Lamb! For this reason they are before the throne of God, and they serve him day and night in his temple, and the one seated on the throne will shelter them. They will never go hungry or be thirsty again, and the sun will not beat down on them, nor any burning heat, because the Lamb in the middle of the throne will shepherd them and lead them to springs of living water, and God will wipe away every tear from their eyes" (Rev 7:9–17).

They are protected by being taken out of the great tribulation to heaven where they are seen praising God for

9. Immediately before this scene, the throne of the Father is indicated to be located above, not on the earth (Rev 6:14–16; cf. Rev 8:1–7).

their deliverance and salvation.[10] The cohesive link should not be missed between Rev 7:9–17 and Jesus's Olivet Discourse concerning the cutting short of the great tribulation: "For then there will be a great tribulation, such as has not occurred since the beginning of the world until now, nor ever will. Unless those days had been cut short, no life [of the elect][11] would have been saved; but for the sake of the elect those days will be cut short" (Matt 24:21–22 NASB). The great tribulation is cut short when Jesus returns to gather his elect before he metes out his judgment (Matt 24:29–31, cf. John 14:1–3).

It is not a coincidence, then, that both groups are viewed together being protected from God's wrath just before the seventh seal is opened. God's wrath does not begin at the start of the seventieth week—it begins when the scroll is *opened*. There is a progression of human depravity before the wrath is unleashed. I agree with J. Webb Mealy's proposal concerning the nature and purpose of the first four seals: "The first four seals (Rev. 6:1–8), for example, far from revealing divine chastisements, reveal the catalysts through which sinful and murderous humanity is brought to witness against itself [i.e. "a certificate of indebtedness"]. The four horsemen thus represent demonic agencies whose release into the arena of nations and societies tempts them to express their true nature."[12] He continues, "The idea that God uses (evil) spirits to accomplish this kind of judgment (i.e. the revelation of true motives) is an old one (cf. Job 2.2,

---

10. For an elaboration on this event, see my exegetical treatment on this text understanding this event as the *result* of the resurrection and the rapture (Kurschner, *Antichrist Before the Day of the Lord*, 57–101).

11. The context clearly indicates that the scope of "life" is referring specifically to the elect, not every single human being alive.

12. Mealy, *After the Thousand Years*, 67; cf. Roller, "Das Buch," 98–113. Mealy notes Paul's similar notion in Col 2:14 concerning *cheirographon*, "record of debts" (LN).

7, 2 Kgs 22.19–23, and the term "satan," i.e. prosecutor). It is also to be found in the eschatology of 2 Thess. 2.8–12."[13] In God's sovereign decree, the nations will persecute his saints, only then to punish those nations. To put the narrative in progressive terms: the first four seals *prove* the guilty for God's wrath (Rev 6:1–8). The fifth seal *promises* God's wrath (Rev 6:9–11). The sixth seal *portends* God's wrath (Rev 6:12–17). Two groups are *protected* from God's wrath (Rev 7). The seventh seal *pronounces* God's wrath (Rev 8–9, 15–16).

Revelation 7 then pictures God's simultaneous programs for Israel and the church during Daniel's seventieth week. God does not work with Israel exclusively since he is involved with Gentile saints (e.g. Rev 7:9). If God does not work simultaneously with Israel and the church during the seventieth week, how can it be claimed in principle that he will work with Gentiles as Rev 7 demonstrates—since Dan 9:24–27 does not mention Gentile saints?

Finally, there are two related passages in Revelation that require comment. First, Rev 12:17–18 reads, "So the dragon became enraged at the woman [Israel] and went away to make war on the rest of her children, those who keep God's commandments and hold to the testimony about Jesus [church saints]. And the dragon stood on the sand of the seashore." This passage is set in the context after the midpoint of the seventieth week when Satan possesses the Beast "having great wrath," who will first pursue the "woman," the Jewish remnant (cf. 2 Thess 2:1–9). His plan is thwarted (Rev 12:13–16), and he turns to pursue his second object of hatred, the church saints: "those who keep God's commandments and hold to the testimony about Jesus" (Rev 12:17, cf. Rev 13:9–10).[14] This additional passage portrays the

13. Mealy, *After the Thousand Years*, 67.

14. Revelation 12:1—15:4 is a major parenthetical section that pauses the "sets of seven" narrative to describe a panoramic view of the kingdom conflict between Satan and God, particularly describing

juxtaposition of two redemptive groups, a Jewish remnant [Israel] and the church saints, with both groups being seen on earth during the time of the Beast's great tribulation before God's wrath begins.[15] The last related passage concerns the beautiful description of both groups representing the whole people of God in the consummation: "[The New Jerusalem] has a massive, high wall with twelve gates, with twelve angels at the gates, and the names of the *twelve tribes of the nation of Israel* [representing Israel] are written on the gates. There are three gates on the east side, three gates on the north side, three gates on the south side and three gates on the west side. The wall of the city has twelve foundations, and on them are the *twelve names of the twelve apostles of the Lamb* [representing the church]" (Rev 21:12–14). Not only will God work with both entities during the seventieth week, but this last passage shows God working with both groups simultaneously in the millennium and beyond.

In summary, God worked with Israel and the church in the past and continues to do so up to this day. He will also work with them both in the future during the seventieth week of Daniel.[16]

---

the Beast's previous activities during the great tribulation that was anticipated by the fourth and fifth seals.

15. Pretribulationists often claim that the mention of "saints" or "those who keep God's commandments and hold to the testimony about Jesus" refer to so-called post-rapture "tribulation saints." They believe that this group was saved after the pretribulation rapture and should not be considered part of the church. This is an inference without biblical support in order to explain the presence of believers during the great tribulation. It is a distinction based on a theological preconceived notion and not on actual exegetical support.

16. For a related line of reasoning, see Appendix 2, "Church Mysteries Extend into the Seventieth Week," where I outline church mysteries that are fulfilled during the future seventieth week of Daniel.

Conclusion

In Part 1, I critiqued the ecclesiastical presupposition. In Chapter 1, I situated this presupposition within the framework of dispensational theology, describing its varieties and distinctives. In Chapter 2, I examined Daniel's prophecy in Dan 9:24–27 as a foundational proof text for traditional pretribulationism, the belief that the church will be excluded from the seventieth week of Daniel. It was concluded that it is mistaken to understand that since the prophecy was made to Israel, the church cannot be present on earth during its fulfillment. In Chapter 3, I critiqued the related claim that God does not work with Israel and the church at the same time. I argued rather that God has worked with Israel and the church at the same time in the past, he does in the present, and will do so in the future. Key Old Testament messianic prophecies were given to Israel that were fulfilled by Israel at the time when the church was established on earth and continue to be fulfilled in the present church age. The interpreter, then, should not find it surprising that God will work with both Israel and the church in the future during the seven-year period. I explicated biblical evidence that supports that the church will be present along with Israel during the seven-year period. For these reasons, the ecclesiastical presupposition lacks biblical support as a foundational belief. Pretribulationism is based on unsound exegesis and flawed reasoning. God works with both Israel and the church simultaneously, while maintaining distinctive purposes for each within his larger redemptive plan. There is diversity within unity. One people of God, realized through remnants from the nations, including Israel.

In Part 2, I will critique the second pretribulation foundation, the Parousia presupposition. This presupposition maintains that the rapture is disconnected from the second coming. It will be shown instead that the New Testament authors linked the rapture with the beginning of the second coming. The rapture is not equated with the second coming, but *belongs* to it. The resurrection and rapture will be the overture to the unified extended-whole of the second coming of Jesus.

Part 2

THE PAROUSIA PRESUPPOSITION: THE RAPTURE IS NOT PART OF THE SECOND COMING

In Part 2, I will examine the Parousia presupposition. This is the other foundational presupposition that operates within pretribulation rapture theology. The Parousia presupposition disconnects the rapture (and resurrection) from the second coming. The Parousia presupposition creates an additional hermeneutic filter for passages addressing the rapture and the second coming (i.e. the Parousia).[1] Pretribulationism maintains that the rapture and second coming are separated from each other by the seven years of Daniel's seventieth week: the rapture for the church and the second coming for Israel. There are no Old Testament prophecies, they argue, that will be fulfilled before the seventieth week—that is, during the church age. The prophecies will be fulfilled *during* the seventieth week. For this reason, pretribulation theology maintains the rapture will be a signless, imminent event for the church.

---

1. I will use the terms *second coming* and *Parousia* interchangeably in this volume. I justify this use below.

In Part 2, I will demonstrate that the Parousia presupposition is deeply flawed. I will argue that the rapture belongs to the second coming; and more specifically, that the second parousia of Christ begins with the rapture and resurrection. In Chapter 4, I will describe key terms that the New Testament authors used to describe the unified extended-whole of the second coming. In Chapter 5, I examine several pretribulation notions that purport to disconnect the rapture from the second coming. In Chapter 6, I will contend that the second coming does not begin with the battle of Armageddon, a common belief among many interpreters. Finally, in Chapter 7, I will round out Part 2 by further arguing that the second coming begins with the rapture and resurrection of the saints, thereby establishing that there is no gap between the rapture and the beginning of the second coming of Christ. Consequently, when Jesus returns, the rapture and God's eschatological wrath will happen back to back.

Chapter 4

DESCRIPTIONS OF THE RETURN OF JESUS

In Chapter 4, I will begin to critique the second of two pretribulation foundations—the Parousia presupposition—which disconnects the rapture from the second coming. However, we need to become familiar with key terms that describe Jesus's return that will help us establish a unified, composite picture of this glorious event. This fuller-orbed description will inform our main critique in the following chapters.

Jesus is coming *again*. The author of Hebrews emphasizes this promise by using an ordinal number: "so also, after Christ was offered once to bear the sins of many, to those who eagerly await him he will appear a second [*deuteros*] time, not to bear sin but to bring salvation" (Heb 9:28, cf. 10:37). The most general theological expression that Christians use to describe this event is *the return of Jesus*. The biblical authors employed many descriptive terms to portray this event.[1]

---

1. The following terms possess semantic ranges that are used in different contexts other than the return of Christ. So the interpreter must be careful not to assume that these are technical terms denoting

John records this promise using the common Greek verb *erchomai*, which is commonly rendered *to come, go,* or *be brought* (BDAG): "And if I go and make ready a place for you, I will come [*erchomai*] again and take you to be with me, so that where I am you may be too" (John 14:3). Only a few days earlier on the Mount of Olives, Jesus delivered to these same disciples a discourse about his return: "Then the sign of the Son of Man will appear in heaven, and all the tribes of the earth will mourn. They will see the Son of Man arriving [*erchomai*] on the clouds of heaven with power and great glory" (Matt 24:30). Luke records an angelic pronouncement: "Men of Galilee, why do you stand here looking up into the sky? This same Jesus who has been taken up from you into heaven will come [*erchomai*] back in the same way you saw him go into heaven" (Acts 1:11). The apostle Paul, in prohibiting certain actions before Jesus returns, writes, "So then, do not judge anything before the time. Wait until the Lord comes [*erchomai*]. He will bring to light the hidden things of darkness and reveal the motives of hearts. Then each will receive recognition from God" (1 Cor 4:5). The book of Revelation depicts the event in prophetic progress: "Look! He is returning [*erchomai*] with the clouds, and every eye will see him" (Rev 1:7a, cf. 22:20).

There is another Greek term, *hēkō*, used in the book of Revelation that represents the idea *to come to, to reach, to arrive* (LN). Referring to Jesus's return in this context, it likely takes a more forceful sense: "Therefore, remember what you received and heard, and obey it, and repent. If you do not wake up, I will come [*hēkō*] like a thief, and you will never know at what hour I will come [*hēkō*] against you" (Rev 3:3). Paul uses the verb *katabainō* that represents linear movement *to move down, to come down, to go down, to descend* (LN), describing Jesus returning from heaven downward to the

---

the return of Christ in every instance they are used in the Bible.

sky where he will meet and be united with his people: "For the Lord himself will come down [*katabainō*] from heaven with a shout of command, with the voice of the archangel, and with the trumpet of God, and the dead in Christ will rise first" (1 Thess 4:16). There is no single term that can capture the fuller description of Jesus's multifaceted return, and as we shall see, there are more. Depending on the context, one author can use a term to denote the unified extended-whole of his return, while another author can use the same term to emphasize, for example, the initial point of his appearing. The interpreter must be careful to observe how these terms are being used in their specific contexts. Various elements in the context will constrain a term's meaning. While words carry a range of meanings within a semantic range, we do not know the specific meaning until it is used in a specific contextual environment.

Theophany and the Day of the Lord

Before we continue to discuss more significant terms relating to Christ's return, we will consider the broader theological notion of a *theophany* and its relationship with the day of the Lord.[2] When we talk about the return of Jesus, we are in essence speaking of a theophany, a term that comes from the Greek compound words for "god" and "to appear" and refers to events portraying God manifesting himself visibly or audibly. An example of this is found in the quintessential apocalyptic breaking of the sixth seal, which causes celestial disturbances, a great earthquake, and the sky splitting apart. This theophany is fearfully witnessed by the wicked:

> The sky was split apart like a scroll being rolled up, and every mountain and island was moved from its place. Then the kings of the earth, the very important people,

2. The following is a significant expansion of my discussion in *Antichrist Before the Day of the Lord*, 105–14, 171–77.

> the generals, the rich, the powerful, and everyone, slave and free, hid themselves in the caves and among the rocks of the mountains. They said to the mountains and to the rocks, "Fall on us and hide us from the face of the one who is seated on the throne and from the wrath of the Lamb." (Rev 6:14–16)

Throughout history God has revealed himself through creation, the Spirit, Christophanies, angels, prophets, dreams, visions, consciences, and ultimately the incarnate Son of God, Jesus. God uses any means to communicate his will, even through a donkey (Num 22:21–35). One day, though, there will be a divine revelation in which our Lord appears in the clouds to bestow glorified bodies and deliver his people. That day will be a joyful manifestation for those who belong to God, but a horrific, heart-stopping judgment for those who do not. In the garden of Eden, Adam and Eve were the first humans to witness God's judgment. He graciously offered them paradise and intimate fellowship, but their faithfulness did not last. Our primal parents sinned. Soon after Adam and Eve sinned by eating from the Tree of the Knowledge of Good and Evil, God was described as "walking in the garden in the cool of the day." This portrayal has been interpreted as God cavalierly taking a stroll even as our first parents had just sinned, bringing down all humanity. In recent decades, a growing number of Old Testament scholars have examined more closely that the translation should not be rendered this way. The New English Translation contains a similar expression, "moving about in the orchard at the breezy time." Most traditional translations also render it this way; for example, the New American Standard Bible has, "They heard the sound of the LORD God walking in the garden in the cool of the day, and the man and his wife hid themselves from the presence of the LORD God among the trees of the garden" (Gen 3:8). The traditional rendering is not likely the best choice because of the context of impending judgment.

We have gained new understanding of this passage based on insights from ancient Near Eastern languages. A better rendering is "shekinah-judgment of the day" or "in the wind of the storm."[3] These renderings make better sense because the Genesis passage is found in the genre of a judgment oracle, consisting of elements such as the breaking of God's commands, the sound of the Lord God approaching, the shameful disobedient fleeing and hiding from God, and the Lord consequently pronouncing punishment on them. This is a *theophany*, and in this case, a judgment theophany. Experiencing a theophany does not mean someone is able to see God's spirit or essential being; they cannot (1 John 4:12). Rather, theophanies are supernatural occurrences, such as the glory of the divine presence, an angel of the Lord, or his spoken words. Theophanies reveal and conceal. God has revealed his glory in brightness like lightning and has concealed it through darkened clouds. If God were to reveal his whole self, sinners would immediately perish from exposure to his pure holiness (e.g. Exod 33:20). Jeffrey J. Niehaus offers this translation of the Genesis verse, bringing out the theophanic elements:

> Then the man and his wife heard the thunder of Yahweh God going back and forth in the garden in the wind of the storm, and they hid from Yahweh God among the trees of the garden (Gen 3:8).

Niehaus remarks, "Such was the first Sinai-like theophany—the first storm theophany when God appeared as Judge of his guilty people."[4] Regarding this verse, the New English Translation comments that if this theophanic judgment rendering is correct, then,

> God is not pictured as taking an afternoon stroll through

3. On *ruakh* see Niehaus, *God at Sinai*, 157; cf. Kline, "Primal Parousia," 245–80.

4. Niehaus, *God at Sinai*, 18.

> the orchard, but as coming in a powerful windstorm to confront the man and woman with their rebellion. In this case ["sound of the Lord"] may refer to God's thunderous roar, which typically accompanies his appearance in the storm to do battle or render judgment (e.g. see Ps. 29).

One of the most common terms found in the Old and New Testament for Christ's eschatological, theophanic return is "the day of the Lord" (Hebrew: *yôm yhwh*; Greek: *hē hēmera tou kyriou*). God's judgment of Adam and Eve in the garden is a prototypical day of the Lord, giving us context for later theophanic episodes. This microcosmic event has been coined the "primal parousia" (first presence).[5] In this, we can begin to appreciate a biblical continuity of God's theophanic program, a continuity reaching all the way back to the garden and one day fully manifesting on the global-eschatological scale.

An eschatological parallel exists between our first parents, who desired to be autonomous from God, and the autonomy-seeking nations that will rebel when the Lord returns. Additional theophanies have been realized between these two theophanies. While the return of the Lord will be the *par excellence* of theophanies (Matt 24:30, 1 Thess 4:16, 2 Thess 1:7, Titus 2:13, Rev 1:7), there have been a variety of theophanies at decisive moments in Israel's redemptive history, including Jacob wrestling with God (Gen 32:22–32), Moses at the burning bush (Exod 3), the Exodus (Exod 13:21–22), God at Sinai (Exod 19), the news of the birth of Samson (Judg 13), and the calling of prophets (Isa 6, Ezek 1). Angels and figures in human form have also manifested within biblical history; it is correct to understand many of these instances as pre-incarnate appearances of Christ (i.e. "christophanies"). The New Testament is likewise punctuated with theophanies at key redemptive moments. We think of the

5. Kline, "Primal Parousia," 245–70.

unique and ultimate theophany of Jesus's incarnation (John 1:14), Jesus's baptism (Mark 1:9–11), the Transfiguration (Matt 17:1–8), Paul's conversion (Acts 9), the sending of the Holy Spirit (John 16:7, Acts 2), and God's dwelling in Zion with his people for eternity (Rev 21:1–4, cf. Isa 2:3, Joel 3:17, Zech 14:16–21). These theophanies reflect God's redemptive purposes to judge, deliver, and seek to dwell with his people.

Concerning the description of the day of the Lord, some explanations will acquaint us with this common expression. The personal name for God is *Yahweh*, which is the Hebrew term behind the English word "Lord" in the expression "the day of the Lord." Many English translations render *Yahweh* with small capital letters (LORD), not to give emphasis, but to distinguish God's name from the regular lowercase "Lord," which is the Hebrew term *adonai*. The Hebrew word for "day" is *yôm*. The term in our context refers to a period larger in scope than a mere twenty-four-hour day. *Yôm* contains about a dozen different meanings in the Old Testament, so context plays the key role (HALOT). It refers to a literal twenty-four-hour day when it is associated with a number (e.g. "three days") or certain other qualifiers such as "full day," "each day," "every day," "a full day," and "the Sabbath day." In contrast, the prophets often used "day" to denote the epochal time when God would break into history in glory and judgment, bringing the ungodly to account (see the list below). They describe this eschatological period as decisive, yet extended, unfolding over time. The book of Revelation reveals that the fifth trumpet judgment will last five months (Rev 9:5, 10) and the seventh trumpet will unfold for an indeterminate number of "days" (Rev 10:7).

The "day of the Lord" is not the only biblical expression that refers to God's eschatological judgment upon the ungodly. The Old and New Testaments use about twenty variant forms:[6]

6. The expression "day of the Lord" (*yôm yhwh*) is found in the

- the day of the Lord's sacrifice (Zeph 1:8)
- the day of the Lord's wrath (Zeph 1:18)
- in those days (Joel 3:1)
- the day (1 Thess 5:4)
- the great Day (Jude 6)
- that day (Isa 2:11)
- judgment day (Isa 10:3)
- the day of his burning anger (Isa 13:13)
- the day of vengeance (Isa 34:8)
- a day is coming for the Lord (Zech 14:1)
- unique day (Zech 14:7)
- the harvest (Matt 13:39)
- the coming of the Son of Man (Matt 24:37)
- the days of the Son of Man (Luke 17:26)
- the day of wrath (Rom 2:5)
- the last day (John 12:48)
- the day of judgment (2 Pet 2:9)
- the day of God (2 Pet 3:12)
- the great day of God (Rev 16:14)

We must be careful, then, not to fallaciously think that if a passage does not contain the exact expression *the day of the Lord* (and other terms under consideration in this chapter), it cannot apply to the concept of God's eschatological judgment.[7] As seen above, the biblical prophets and writers

---

Old Testament 16 times: Joel 1:15, 2:1, 11, 2:31, 3:14, Obad 1:15, Isa 13:6, 9, Ezek 13:5, Amos 5:18(x2), 20, Zeph 1:7, 14(x2), Mal 4:5. See also Isa 2:12, 13:13, 34:8, Ezek 7:19, 30:3, Zeph 1:8, 18, 2:2–3, Zech 14:7, Lam 1:12, 2:1.

7. This is a form of the word-concept fallacy, also known as the theological-concept fallacy, an assumption that studying a single word or phrase corresponds to having studied the entire biblical concept. The fallacy is also known as the "concordance method" of interpretation. One should not simply open up a concordance and finger down the page looking for instances of a single word and stop there. Doing so can be a beginning point for study, but there is an important difference between studying a biblical concept and studying the range of meanings of a single word. For example, if we want to learn what the Bible teaches about love, it would be a mistake to restrict our study only

had the flexibility of literary expression. These expressions may denote the complete day of the Lord or some stage within it, such as the inception, consummation, or other aspects, depending on their respective contexts. In other words, every passage referring to the day of the Lord contributes to the larger picture. For instance, Joel 2:30–31 and Rev 6:17 use expressions focusing on the *impending* wrath of God, while Rev 16:14 contains an expression drawing attention to the later *climactic* judgment of the battle of Armageddon.

All this judgment discussion about the day of the Lord may give the impression that judgment will be the only characteristic of this day. However, the same prophets who spoke of eschatological judgment also prophesied that this "day" would encompass future hope, redemption, and millennial blessings for the righteous (e.g. Isa 27, 40–66, Mic 4:6–8, Obad 15–17, Jer 30:8–9, Zeph 3:9–20, Zech 14). My emphasis on judgment is not meant to minimize the importance of the millennial blessings and God's glorious goal to dwell with his people.

Parousia (*Coming, Arrival, Presence*)

Having discussed theophanies and the day of the Lord, we turn to the important—and often misunderstood—term

---

to the word *agapē* because there are many terms describing different aspects of love. We need to take Scripture in a contextual sense and recognize synonyms and other similar phrases that describe a concept rather than collapsing an entire concept into a single term. Moisés Silva (*Biblical Words and Their Meaning*, 27) gives this additional example: "A very important passage on the subject of hypocrisy is Isaiah 1:10–15, but the student suckled at the concordance would never find [the word *hypocrisy*]; instead, he would come to an unrefined understanding of the topic." See also Kurschner, "Illegitimate Totality Transfer," 70–89; Carson, *Exegetical Fallacies*, 27–64. Therefore, we must be careful not to assume if a passage lacks the exact expression "day of the Lord," it must not refer to God's eschatological judgment. Biblical passages typically contain descriptive language of the day of the Lord without using the exact term or expression.

parousia. Pretribulationism and posttribulationism have framed the relationship between the rapture and the second coming in either/or terms. Pretribulationists believe that the rapture and the second coming are disconnected from each other, while posttribulationists believe they are identical. The prewrath view offers a third way to understand their relationship. The rapture *belongs* to the second coming. It is a subset to the larger extended event.

While I will focus more on the term *parousia* and its relationship to the rapture in Chapter 7, I want to make some preliminary comments on this term. The Greek term *parousia* means "the state of being present at a place, *presence*" or "an arrival as the first stage in presence, *coming, advent*" (BDAG). The terms "second coming" and "second advent" refer namely to Jesus's arrival and continuing presence among us. Thus, the Greek term *parousia* was fitting for New Testament writers when describing Jesus's future arrival and presence. It is the word Matthew used in his gospel when recording the disciples' question in Matt 24:3: "As he was sitting on the Mount of Olives, his disciples came to him privately and said, 'Tell us, when will these things happen? And what will be the sign of your coming [*parousia*] and of the end of the age?'" In the New Testament, the term is used twenty-four times, always in the singular.[8] The New Testament authors spoke of a single future Parousia, not two future ones (the plural in Koine Greek is *parousiai*). Seventeen times it is used prophetically of our Lord's second coming, including four instances in Matt 24 (the only instances recorded in the Gospels). In secular Greek, the term *parousia* could refer to the arrival of an important person (such as a king) or of a hidden divinity revealing his power. It is befitting that

8. Matt 24:3, 27, 37, 39; 1 Cor 15:23, 16:17; 2 Cor 7:6–7, 10:10; Phil 1:26, 2:12; 1 Thess 2:19, 3:13, 4:15, 5:23; 2 Thess 2:1, 8–9; James 5:7–8; 2 Pet 1:16, 3:4, 12; 1 John 2:28.

Matthew applies this term to Christ's return since there is a royal motif in his gospel. Jesus will manifest himself when he returns, making his presence felt through the revelation of the day-of-the-Lord judgments. Christians are told to make Jesus's Parousia the object of their expectation. For example, Paul states that the second coming of Christ is the believer's hope: "For who is our hope or joy or crown to boast of before our Lord Jesus at his coming [*parousia*]? Is it not of course you?" (1 Thess 2:19; cf. 1 Thess 3:13, 4:15, 5:23, 2 Thess 2:1, 8). James exhorts the believer to have patience as they wait for the second coming: "So be patient, brothers and sisters, until the Lord's return [*parousia*]. Think of how the farmer waits for the precious fruit of the ground and is patient for it until it receives the early and late rains. You also be patient and strengthen your hearts, for the Lord's return [*parousia*] is near" (Jas 5:7–8). Peter urges soberness concerning God's coming wrath as believers should wait for his second coming since it will involve back-to-back deliverance and judgment: "while waiting for and hastening the coming [*parousia*] of the day of God? Because of this day, the heavens will be burned up and dissolve, and the celestial bodies will melt away in a blaze!" (2 Pet 3:12). Finally, John heeds the church to possess steadfast faithfulness to Christ as they wait for his second coming: "And now, little children, remain in him, so that when he appears we may have confidence and not shrink away from him in shame when he comes back [*parousia*]" (1 John 2:28). These passages indicate that the church will be on earth up to the beginning of his second Parousia.

The Lord's second coming/Parousia will be a unified, extended event. That is, it will not be a simple, instantaneous event. The scope will include a manifold of events that will fulfill divine purposes. We can liken it to Jesus's first coming. When we think of his first coming, we do not think exclusively of his birth. Indeed, his birth was his arrival, but his subsequent presence included his upbringing, teaching ministry, miracles, death, burial, resurrection, and ascension. It was a unified, extended event to fulfill divine purposes through the Son. Similarly, the second coming will *begin* with Jesus's arrival in the clouds to resurrect the dead in Christ and rapture them along with believers who are still alive at that time (1 Thess 4:13–18), but it will not conclude there. The biblical writers often emphasized the arrival aspect of the Parousia because they wanted to induce godly living in their listeners. But it would be a mistake to think they viewed the Parousia as limited only to his glorious appearing in the sky. His coming will encompass major events such as the day of the Lord's wrath, bringing the remnant of Israel to salvation, the battle of Armageddon, and the reclaiming of his earthly regal rule that will extend throughout the millennium.

In summary, (1) the term *parousia* means an arrival and a continued presence, and thus it refers to a unified, extended period, not an instantaneous event, (2) the rapture belongs to the second coming as it is a subset to the larger extended event, (3) the biblical writers were consistent with Jesus in teaching that the Parousia is the church's hope and expectation as they will be on earth when it begins with the rapture followed by the day of the Lord's wrath, (4) Christ's Parousia will be realized through his roles of deliverer, judge, and king.[9]

9. The apostle Paul describes a specific relationship between the Parousia and the kingdom in 1 Cor 15:24–28. Paul states that when the series of resurrections are accomplished, Christ will "reign until" all his enemies, especially death, are defeated. He will hand over the kingdom to God the Father when everything is put into subjection. After the day-of-the-Lord's judgments, his Parousia (i.e. his presence) will extend his rule over the physical glorified kingdom, eventuating in all enemies being eliminated. Accordingly, his Parousia will not be an instantaneous event; it will be a multi-phased, unified extended-whole in which God will fulfill his divine purposes: "*Then* the Son himself will be subjected to the one who subjected everything to him,

The Parousia as an Extended Event

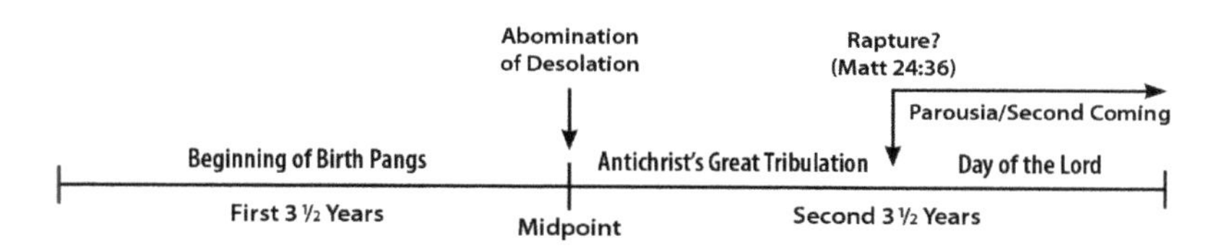

Apokalypsis (*Revelation*), Apokalyptō (*to Reveal*)

The next word group reflects the *revealing* aspect of Jesus's return. Pretribulationism claims that the rapture and the revelation occur at different chronological points in time. The revelation (*apokalypsis*) of Christ, it is argued, will be known to all the world at the end of the seventieth week when Jesus comes with his saints at the battle of Armageddon (where pretribulationists also place the second coming/ Parousia). For example, Gerald B. Stanton writes, "We see clearly that the rapture is not identical with the revelation, commonly called the second coming of Christ. These are two distinct events."[10] Stanton is correct to say they are not identical, but he also means that they are separated from each other by an interval of seven years. When the glorious revelation of Jesus Christ occurs, the rapture is thought to have already happened seven years earlier. This is mistaken for the following reasons.

The Greek noun *apokalypsis* means "making fully known" and rendered commonly as *revelation or disclosure* (BDAG). Similarly, the verb form *apokalyptō* means "to be

so that God may be all in all."

10. Stanton, "Doctrine of Imminency," 223, cf. 256–68.

fully known" and can be rendered *reveal, disclose, bring to light, or make fully known* (BDAG). The New Testament authors used the term *apokalypsis* to convey the aspect of Jesus's return that will reveal his purpose in delivering the godly and meting out judgment upon the ungodly. The revelation of Christ is an event that will happen while the church is still on earth, and we are exhorted to wait for it. This glorious event is not something that will happen seven years after the rapture. For example, Paul explicitly teaches the Corinthian church to wait for it: "so that you do not lack any spiritual gift as you *wait* for the revelation [*apokalypsis*] of our Lord Jesus Christ" (1 Cor 1:7). In the very next verse, Paul links his exhortation to God's promise that his church will be strengthened in order to be blameless: "He will also strengthen you to the end, so that you will be blameless on the day of our Lord Jesus Christ" (1 Cor 1:8). The rapture, then, is linked to the revelation of Christ, *which is what will make the rapture possible in the first place*. The rapture will therefore happen at Jesus's revelation.[11] Paul also connects the suffering of the church that will continue until Jesus's revelation: "If indeed we suffer with him so we may also be glorified with him. For I consider that our present sufferings cannot even be compared to the glory that will be revealed [*apokalyptō*] to us. For the creation eagerly waits for the revelation [*apokalypsis*] of the sons of God" (Rom 8:17–19, cf. 1 Cor 3:13). This passage makes no sense in the pretribulation framework. Pretribulationists believe that the church will not be suffering when the revelation of Christ occurs because they believe the church to have been raptured to heaven seven years earlier. Moreover, in Paul's second letter to the Thessalonians, he speaks of both the revelation of Jesus and the revelation of the man of lawlessness (i.e. the Antichrist).

11. It should also be noted that Paul identifies the revelation of Jesus as the "day of our Lord Jesus Christ" (1 Cor 1:8).

In 2 Thess 1:7, he writes, "and to you who are being afflicted to give rest together with us at the revelation [*apokalypsis*] of the Lord Jesus from heaven with his mighty angels." This is another passage that creates a contradiction in the pretribulation framework. Paul is teaching that Christians will be given relief at the revelation (*apokalypsis*), which indicates that they will be on earth being persecuted up to the revelation of Christ. It makes no sense, then, to locate the revelation of Christ seven years after the rapture. A few verses further, Paul specifies—not once, but twice—that the revelation of the man of lawlessness will occur *before* Jesus returns:

> Let no one deceive you in any way. For that day will not arrive until first the apostasy comes and the man of lawlessness is revealed [*apokalyptō*], the son of destruction (2 Thess 2:3).

> [A]nd then the lawless one will be revealed [*apokalyptō*], whom the Lord will destroy by the breath of his mouth and wipe out by the manifestation [*epiphaneia*] of his arrival [*parousia*] (2 Thess 2:8).

Comparing these two verses demonstrates that the church and the man of lawlessness will be on earth simultaneously when Christ's revelation begins. In other words, the revelation of the man of lawlessness will occur first, and then Christ will return to destroy him.[12] The apostle Paul shows nothing of an intervening gap between Jesus's coming for his church at the rapture and his revelation. Instead, Paul writes that the coming for the church will happen at Jesus's

---

12. In the book of Romans, Paul instructs that when Jesus's revelation takes place, the wicked will be judged: "But because of your stubbornness and your unrepentant heart, you are storing up wrath for yourselves in the day of wrath and revelation [*apokalypsis*] of God's judgment" (Rom 2:5, my translation). The pretribulation framework incoherently places the judgment seven years earlier than the revelation.

revelation, and we are to wait for it with eager anticipation while enduring trials of various sorts.

Turning to Peter, we see that he is consistent with the apostle Paul on the matter of trials for the church that will continue up to the glorious revelation of Christ:

> Who by God's power are protected through faith for a salvation ready to be revealed [*apokalyptō*] in the last [*eschatos*] time. This brings you great joy, although you may have to suffer for a short time in various trials. Such trials show the proven character of your faith, which is much more valuable than gold—gold that is tested by fire, even though it is passing away—and will bring praise and glory and honor when Jesus Christ is revealed [*apokalypsis*]. You have not seen him, but you love him. You do not see him now but you believe in him, and so you rejoice with an indescribable and glorious joy. (1 Pet 1:5-8)

Peter unequivocally explains that the church will be on earth, undergoing suffering, when Jesus's revelation takes place. He exhorts the church to persevere from this "short time in various trials" up to the revelation, which will be a time to "rejoice with an indescribable and glorious joy." Thus, when Jesus's *apokalypsis* begins to take place, the rapture of God's people will happen. Peter continues to exhort the church to "set your hope" upon the revelation of Christ: "Therefore, get your minds ready for action by being fully sober, and set your hope completely on the grace that will be brought to you at the revelation [*apokalypsis*] of Jesus Christ" (1 Pet 1:13, see also Titus 2:13, where Paul instructs the church to set its hope on the "glorious appearing" of Christ). Peter makes the counter-intuitive exhortation to rejoice in the face of persecution, because it is short-lived: "But rejoice in the degree that you have shared in the sufferings of Christ, so that in the revelation [*apokalypsis*] of his glory you may also rejoice and be glad" (1 Pet 4:13). Peter joins himself to his fellow believers who are suffering for the name of Christ and recognizes that he, too, will experience glory at the revelation: "So as your fellow elder and a witness of Christ's sufferings and as one who shares in the glory that will be revealed [*apokalyptō*], I urge the elders among you" (1 Pet 5:1). Peter then identifies the time of the revelation with the glorious visible appearing of Jesus: "Then when the Chief Shepherd appears [*phaneroō*], you will receive the crown of glory that never fades away" (1 Pet 5:4). Below we will pick up the word group related to *phaneroō* that means "visible appearing."

Finally, Jesus describes his revelation as an immediate two-fold event: The righteous will be delivered and, that same day, the judgment of the wicked begins. These will be back-to-back events *without any intervening period*: "It will be the same on the day the Son of Man is revealed [*apokalyptō*]" (Luke 17:30, see esp. Luke 17:20—18:8). Certainly, there is the event when Jesus and his heavenly armies are seen in the sky: "Then I saw heaven opened and here came a white horse! The one riding it was called 'Faithful' and 'True,' and with justice he judges and goes to war" (Rev 19:11). However, this latter passage is part of the unified extended return of Jesus. The battle of Armageddon occurs later, after the rapture and resurrection and after the trumpet and bowl judgments. The final battle is just that—*final*— after God executes his wrath through the trumpet and bowl judgments.[13] Most of the passages examined above describe the *initial* aspect of his revelation, which is why the church is exhorted to persevere in faith and hope up to the point when Jesus is revealed.

In summary, (1) the church will be on earth when the revelation occurs, (2) the church will suffer tribulations until she is given relief at the beginning of Christ's revelation, (3) the coming of Christ *for* his people is linked to the revelation of Jesus, and (4) the church is exhorted to persevere in faith

13. See Chapter 6, "The Second Coming Does Not Begin with Armageddon."

and hope to bring glory and honor at the revelation of Christ. In short, the pretribulation understanding of the relationship between the rapture and Christ's revelation is incoherent. The revelation of Christ *is* the church's hope.

The Revelation of the Antichrist and Jesus Christ

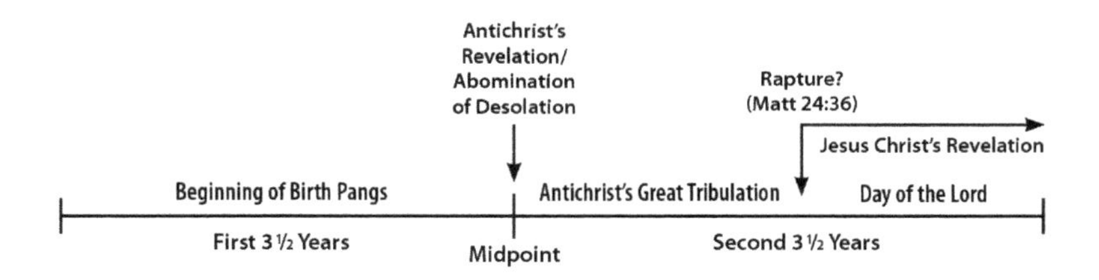

Epiphaneia (*Appearing*), Phaneroō (*to Appear*), Epiphanēs (*Glorious*)

Pretribulationists, similarly, locate the "glorious appearing" (*epiphaneia*) of Christ, not at the time of the rapture, but at the end of the seventieth week with the battle of Armageddon.[14] For instance, J. N. Darby writes,

> [. . .] I certainly apprehend that the period spoken of in the [book of] Revelation (or from chap. 4) is the interval between the removal of the church from the place of testimony, and the manifestation of it in a glorious testimony [. . .].[15]

Tim LaHaye also writes,

> There are no signs for the rapture. All signs of the Lord's return relate to His glorious appearing. Therefore, you must subtract at least the seven-year Tribulation period when thinking about the rapture.[16]

14. Some translations render *epiphaneia* as "manifestation."
15. Darby, *Letters*, 132.
16. LaHaye, "Twelve Reasons," 443. LaHaye's essay, "Twelve

In this section, I will explain why this is a false distinction. The "appearing" word group emphasizes the *visionary* aspect of Jesus's return. What was physically veiled will be visibly manifested. The noun *epiphaneia* means "to appear to someone or at some place" and rendered *to appear, appearance,* or *appearing* (LN). In the first-century Greek world, the term could be used for a "sudden manifestation of a hidden divinity, either in the form of a personal appearance, or by some deed of power or oracular communication by which its presence is made known" (BDAG). The term connotes a *splendid* manifestation. In Paul's exhortation to Timothy to fight the good fight of the faith, he orders him, "[O]bey this command without fault or failure *until* the appearing [*epiphaneia*] of our Lord Jesus Christ" (1 Tim 6:14). Paul therefore expects the church to be on earth when the appearing occurs. This contradicts the pretribulation belief that the appearing will happen seven years later once the church has already been raptured. While the appearing of Christ will bring deliverance for the church, Paul also links the appearing with judgment: "I solemnly charge you before God and Christ Jesus, who is going to judge the living and the dead, and by his appearing [*epiphaneia*] and his kingdom" (2 Tim 4:1). A few verses further, Paul, in unmistakable terms, instructs the church to look for Jesus's appearing when God rewards the righteous: "Finally the crown of righteousness is reserved for me. The Lord, the righteous Judge, will award it to me in that day—and not to me only, but also to all who

---

Reasons Why This Could Be the Terminal Generation" is characteristic of pretribulation literature because pretribulationists maintain that signs are only for "the Jews" and not also for the church. LaHaye devotes most of his essay to explaining why Jesus is likely to return in this generation, only at the end of his essay to alert the reader of the obligatory pretribulation qualification: "Do not forget, we have been talking about Jesus's glorious appearing" (443). Popular pretribulation literature seems to be fixated on current signs, while at the same time insisting that Jesus's return is imminent.

have set their affection on his appearing [*epiphaneia*]" (2 Tim 4:8). This verse is problematic for pretribulationism for two reasons. First, as the other passages previously showed, it locates the appearing when the church is on *earth* waiting for the Lord. Second, it says that the Lord "will reward the righteous" *at the appearing*. This contradicts the pretribulation belief that the church will be rewarded *before the appearing occurs*.[17] The apostle Paul only knows of two unified comings. The first occurred in Jesus's incarnation: "but now made visible through the appearing [*epiphaneia*] of our Savior Christ Jesus. He has broken the power of death and brought life and immortality to light through the gospel!" (2 Tim 1:10). The second will occur in the future, which is why Paul exhorts the church to "set their affection on his appearing [*epiphaneia*]."

Timothy is not the only person that Paul exhorts to look for Jesus's *epiphaneia*. He writes to Titus, encouraging him to "wait for the blessed hope in the glorious appearing [*epiphaneia*] of our great God and Savior, Jesus Christ" (Titus 2:13). Paul teaches that the church's blessed hope is simply *being* with Jesus. This will happen at the glorious appearing of our Savior, at the rapture. Contrary to pretribulationism, the rapture is not the blessed hope, nor is the blessed hope escape from persecution. In short, Paul teaches that the church will be here for the appearing of Christ.

Paul's final mention of *epiphaneia* is the most significant for our purposes. This was briefly noted above but will be reiterated. Paul describes that the Antichrist will be revealed as being already on earth when the *epiphaneia* of our Lord takes place: "and then the lawless one [i.e. the Antichrist] will be revealed, whom the Lord will destroy by the breath of his mouth and wipe out by the appearing [*epiphaneia*] of his coming [*parousia*]" (2 Thess 2:8). The

17. Pentecost, *Things to Come*, 220–21.

implication is unmistakable: Since Paul teaches that the church will be on earth when the *epiphaneia* begins, it follows that both the church and the Antichrist will be active on earth simultaneously. The church will face the Antichrist before the *epiphaneia* of Christ. This confirms what Paul taught in 2 Thess 2:3 that the church would witness the revelation of the Antichrist. Paul's teaching contradicts the pretribulation understanding that the church will be raptured before the Antichrist arrives. It turns Paul's explicit statement on its head. Only when Christ is revealed at his *epiphaneia* will the church be delivered out of the hands of the Antichrist. Moreover, in 2 Thess 2:8, Paul links the term *epiphaneia* with *parousia:* "by the appearing [*epiphaneia*] of his coming [*parousia*]." This reminds us that Paul is not restricted to using only one term to describe Jesus's future return. The biblical writers used many descriptive terms to capture the multifaceted aspects of this glorious event.

In addition to the noun *epiphaneia*, the verb form occurs in the context of Jesus's return. The Greek verb *phaneroō* means "to cause to become visible" and rendered *to make appear, to make visible,* or *to cause to be seen* (LN). The emphasis of this term is on the initial aspect of Christ's return, that radiant manifestation of our Lord in the sky. For example, the apostle John exhorts believers to abide in Christ until he comes back: "And now, little children, remain in him, so that when he appears [*phaneroō*] we may have confidence and not shrink away from him in shame when he comes back [*parousia*]" (1 John 2:28). John believes that the church will be on earth at the time Jesus appears and thus exhorts us not to be ashamed at his coming (notice that John, consistent with Paul, links Jesus's appearing with the Parousia). John continues to teach that as sinners we will be made pure "just as he is" when he is revealed: "Dear friends, we are God's children now, and what we will be has not yet been revealed [*phaneroō*]. We know that whenever it is revealed [*phaneroō*] we will be like him, because we will see him just as he is" (1 John 3:2). "[E]veryone who has this hope focused on him purifies himself, *just as Jesus is pure*" (1 John 3:3). The rapture and the resurrection will occur at the appearing of Jesus because John links our new transformation to being like Jesus at the time of his appearing. In the same vein, Paul states, "When Christ (who is your life) appears [*phaneroō*] then you too will be revealed in glory with him" (Col 3:4). And Peter teaches that the church will be given her crown of glory when Jesus appears: "Then when the Chief Shepherd appears [*phaneroō*], you will receive the crown of glory that never fades away" (1 Pet 5:4). As noted earlier, in the immediate context, Peter identifies this glorious appearing as occurring at the same time as the revelation of Christ: "So as your fellow elder and a witness of Christ's sufferings and as one who shares in the glory that will be revealed [*apokalyptō*] . . ." (1 Pet 5:1). These descriptions from the biblical writers contradict the pretribulation framework, which locates Jesus's appearing seven years after the rapture toward the end of the seventieth week.

Finally, the adjectival form in this word group is *epiphanēs*, which means "pertaining to being glorious or wonderful, in view of being conspicuous and self-evident" and rendered *glorious, wonderful,* or *marvelous*" (LN). This term is used in contrast to the dark celestial disturbances that will announce the day of the Lord: "The sun will be changed to darkness and the moon to blood *before* the great and glorious [*epiphanēs*] day of the Lord comes" (Acts 2:20). This is consistent with Jesus's teaching that the radiance of the sign of the Son of man will pierce through the darkness of the celestial disturbances for the world to see: "For just like the lightning comes from the east and flashes to the west, so the coming of the Son of Man will be" (Matt 24:27, cf. 24:28–29).

In summary, the word group *phaneroō*, *epiphaneia*, and *epiphanēs* describe the revealing glory-manifestation of Christ. These actions portray, not disconnected events, but complementary actions, providing a stunning, glorious portrayal of Jesus's return. The uses of the terms in this word group teach us five things: (1) the church will be on earth at the time of the appearing of Christ, (2) the appearing and meeting of Christ is the church's blessed hope, (3) the church is encouraged to live in holiness until the appearing and become like Christ when he appears, (4) church saints will be rewarded at the appearing for loving his appearing, and (5) the appearing and revelation of Christ are simultaneous facets of Jesus's second coming for the church. Far from being disconnected from the rapture, the appearing of Christ is a description of the glorious return when Jesus will resurrect and rapture the people of God. The pretribulation understanding is untenable and relies on an artificial distinction that is incompatible with the teachings of the biblical authors. The appearing of Christ *is* the church's hope.

The Appearing/Epiphaneia of Christ

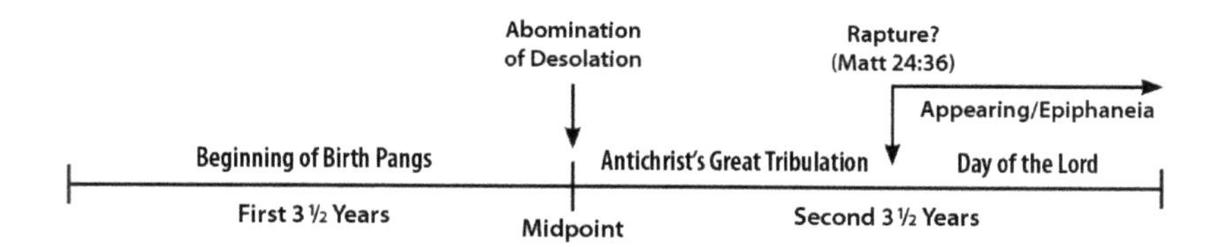

Conclusion

This chapter described many key terms that the biblical authors employed to describe for their audiences on the awesome event of the Lord's return. These meanings depict complementary aspects of his return, providing a stunning, glorious portrayal of Jesus's return as a unified extended event. I also examined the pretribulation understandings of these terms and concluded that they represent mistaken and incoherent distinctions. Having established a composite of Jesus's return, in the next chapter I will continue to focus on critiquing the Parousia presupposition, which disconnects the rapture from the second coming.

Chapter 5

'COME FOR HIS SAINTS' AND 'COME WITH HIS SAINTS'

The previous chapter outlined the terms the biblical authors used to describe the awesome event of the Lord's return. I also critiqued how pretribulation interpreters create false temporal dichotomies. This chapter will continue to examine the second of the two foundational pretribulation presuppositions, the Parousia presupposition. First, I will use a thought-provoking comparison to illustrate the fallacious pretribulation approach. Second, I will continue examining the Parousia presupposition that disconnects the rapture from the second coming/Parousia.[1] This dichotomy is foundational to the pretribulation interpretive framework. This examination establishes that the rapture belongs to the second coming. This conclusion will be consequential as it places the church on earth during the great tribulation but before the day of the Lord's wrath.

1. When I mention the *rapture*, the resurrection is also in view since the two events will occur back to back in conjunction with each other (1 Thess 4:13–18).

'Come for His Saints' and 'Come with His Saints'

As noted, pretribulationism separates the rapture from the second coming with the intervening period of Daniel's seventieth week. I am arguing instead that the biblical evidence supports that the rapture belongs to the extended unified event of the second coming. I will frame my critique around what has become a pretribulation slogan that goes something like this: At the rapture, Christ will come *for* his saints; at the second coming, he will come *with* his saints. Pretribulationist Edward E. Hindson captures this assertion:

> Pretribulationists divide the return of Christ in two main phases: the rapture of the church and the second coming of Christ. In the first aspect, our Lord comes to take His own (the living and the dead) to be with Him. In the second aspect, He returns with His resurrected and raptured saints to win the battle of Armageddon and to establish His kingdom on earth.[2]

This understanding lends to the claim that Jesus's return will occur in two stages—the rapture "coming" and the second "coming"—being separated by seven years. Hindson further argues that "the *dissimilarities* between the rapture passages and the return passages [i.e. second coming] are significant enough to indicate that they are *separate* events" (emphasis his).[3] Similarly, Showers believes, "the Rapture will take place at a different time than the coming of Christ . . . (i.e., the Second Coming)."[4] To support this claim, pretribulationists enumerate several purported "contrasts" between these two events. While more contrasts could be commented on, the following table represents four of the most common found in pretribulation literature.[5]

---

2. Hindson, "Rapture and the Return," 157.

3. Hindson, "Rapture and the Return," 157.

4. Showers, *Maranatha*, 176.

5. E.g. Pentecost, *Things to Come*, 206–207; Walvoord, *Rapture Question*, 2nd ed., 93–95; Feinberg, "Case for the Pretribulation

Table 1.
Pretribulation Contrasts

The Rapture Coming	**The Second Coming**
Jesus will come *for* his church	Jesus will come *with* his church
Jesus comes in the air	Jesus comes to the earth
No signs – imminent	Signs – not imminent
Only his own see him	Every eye will see him

I will comment on each of these four sets of pretribulation contrasts. But I will first demonstrate the flawed nature of these contrasts by illustrating an absurdity of contrasts of my own. In the following table, I have chosen four "contrasts" from the Passion narrative of Jesus recorded from the four Gospels.

Table 2.
Passion Narrative 'Contrasts'

Passion A	**Passion B**
Peter defends Jesus (John 18:10)	Peter denies Jesus (John 18:25–27)
Jesus silent before his accusers (Mark 14:61)	Jesus speaks before his accusers (Mark 14:62)
Jesus carries the cross (John 19:17)	Simon carries the cross (Matt 27:32)
A soldier pierced Jesus's side (John 19:34)	A soldier confessed Jesus as Son of God (Mark 15:39)

Rapture Position," 72, 80–86; Hitchcock, *Could the Rapture Happen Today?*, 78–81; Hindson, "Rapture and the Return," 156–57; Akin, *The Return of Christ*, 56.

If we apply the pretribulation mode of reasoning from Table 1 to the Passion narrative, it would follow that there are *two different* Passions of Jesus. I took selective elements within the same unified Passion narrative and gave the impression that there are two different Passions containing incompatible elements (Passion A and Passion B). Of course, this is absurd, because considering the *contexts* of each element, it shows that they rather complement each other. They depict a single account of a unified extended event of Jesus's one and only Passion. In like manner, pretribulationists skew the biblical portrayal when they posit two different comings of the Lord: "the rapture coming" and "the second coming." The Parousia presupposition lifts events out of context and wrongly pits them against each other, resulting in the misleading notion that the rapture is disconnected from the second coming.[6]

In the remaining part of this chapter, as well as the next two chapters, I will explain why the rapture belongs to the unified event of the second coming. The implication for this cannot be overstated because it fractures the foundation of pretribulationism. If the rapture belongs to the second coming, then passages such as Matt 24:27–31, which place the second coming after the Antichrist's great tribulation, reveal that the church will be on earth during that time.[7] In addition, the Thessalonian letters and the book of Revelation show to have intervening events and signs before the rapture. This implication is why the Parousia presupposition is one of the

---

6. Consequently, pretribulationism divides up the saints of God between two general resurrections: a resurrection for New Testament saints at the rapture and another resurrection occurring at a later point in time for Old Testament saints and so-called tribulation saints; e.g. Pentecost, *Things to Come*, 209.

7. To reiterate, in the prewrath view, the Antichrist's great tribulation is a different event from the day of the Lord's wrath. The latter event will happen *after* the former. The church is not exempt from the Antichrist's great tribulation, but it is exempt (raptured) from God's wrath, commonly known as the day of the Lord.

two major foundational structures within pretribulationism.

Next, I will critique each of the so-called pretribulation contrasting elements by explaining their respective contexts.

Critique of Pretribulation Contrasts

Table 3.
First Contrast

The Rapture Coming	The Second Coming
Jesus will come *for* his church	Jesus will come *with* his church

Of the four contrasts that I will address, this first one is the most frequently cited in pretribulation literature, so I will focus on it the most.[8] I agree with the first element that he will come for his church to rapture her.[9] As for the second element, pretribulation interpreters misunderstand the expression "second coming." What they denote by the second coming is the period at the end of the seventieth week when Jesus and his armies of heaven go to battle at Armageddon. This is a deeply flawed understanding. To be sure, Armageddon *belongs* to the extended event of the second coming of Christ, taking place toward the end of God's eschatological wrath. I will defer this point for Chapter 6, since it deserves its own chapter.

In the previous chapter, I described a host of terms that the biblical authors used to describe the return of Jesus.

8. E.g. Feinberg, "Case for the Pretribulation Rapture Position," 72; Hitchcock, *Could the Rapture Happen Today?*, 78–81; Showers, *Maranatha*, 176–91.

9. Prewrath teaches that the rapture will take place sometime during the second half of the seventieth week of Daniel when the Antichrist's great tribulation is cut short (see Hultberg, *Three Views*; Kurschner, *Antichrist Before the Day of the Lord*; Rosenthal, *Pre-Wrath Rapture*; Van Kampen, *The Sign*).

One of the major terms that I covered was *parousia*. When theologians speak of the "second coming," they are speaking of the second arrival of Christ and his continuing presence. To be sure, the term *parousia* is not a technical term for the second coming since it is also used in non-eschatological contexts.[10] The term *parousia* is a particularly important term used by Matthew in Jesus's Olivet Discourse and in the letters of Paul, Peter, James, and John. More importantly, in their eschatological instructions, Jesus and Paul address the *inception* of the Parousia event. It is not that "Paul addressed the rapture," while "Jesus addressed the second coming," as pretribulationists often contend. What they fail to recognize is that *both* Jesus and Paul are addressing the beginning point of the Parousia, not two different phases of it.

Paul addresses the beginning point of the Parousia by focusing on the resurrection, the rapture, and the beginning of the day of the Lord's wrath, which will happen on the day Christ returns from heaven to the clouds:

> For we tell you this by the word of the Lord, that we who are alive, who are left *until* the coming [*parousia*] of the Lord, will surely not go ahead of those who have fallen asleep. (1 Thess 4:15)

Notice that Paul states "until" (*eis*) the coming (*parousia*) of the Lord, which ties this event to the beginning of the second coming. Similarly, Matthew's presentation of the Olivet Discourse addresses the beginning of the Parousia:

> For just like the lightning comes from the east and flashes to the west, so the coming [*parousia*] of the Son of Man will be. Wherever the corpse is, there the vultures will gather. Immediately after the suffering of those days, the sun will be darkened, and the moon will not give its light; the stars will fall from heaven, and the powers of heaven will be shaken. *Then the sign* of the Son of Man will appear

---

10. E.g. 1 Cor 16:17, 2 Cor 7:6–7, 10:10, Phil 1:26, 2:12.

> in heaven, and all the tribes of the earth will mourn. They will see the Son of Man arriving on the clouds of heaven with power and great glory. And he will send his angels with a loud trumpet blast, and they will gather his elect from the four winds, from one end of heaven to the other (Matt 24:27–31).

Jesus is describing the inception of the Parousia. Jesus gives the *sign* of the Parousia (v. 27): the "lightning," which is his glory. The bright sign will burst through the natural light that went dark as the "powers of heaven are shaken" (vv. 30–31). The disciples' question prompted Jesus's discourse: "Tell us, when will these things happen? And what will be the sign of your coming [*parousia*] and of the end of the age?" (Matt 24:3). Signs are given to *announce* something. When the sign occurs, the Parousia begins. Moreover, Jesus's parables and similitudes (Matt 24:32–51—for instance, the Noahic illustration) explicitly address the beginning of his return, not the end of the day of the Lord's wrath. Noah and his family did not enter the ark after the flood. Jesus's warnings to his disciples to be watchful would be meaningless if he were referring to the *end* of the day of the Lord's wrath. The warnings are intended to exhort disciples to prepare for the Parousia, so they are not caught off guard when it happens. The occurrence of the sign to the Parousia occurs "immediately after" the great tribulation (v. 29). Only then will Christ deliver his people from his day of the Lord's wrath.

Pretribulationism contends that the prophesied events described in Jesus's Olivet Discourse will occur only after the church is raptured; therefore, they maintain that the rapture is not in view in the gathering of the elect portrayed in Matt 24:30–31.[11] Only "Jewish tribulation saints" will experience

11. There is, however, disagreement within pretribulationism on this point. Some interpreters believe that the rapture is described in the Olivet Discourse in Matt 24:36–44, which they claim is a recapitulation of the period before verse 4. The problem is that this view breaks up

the great tribulation, not the church. This is deeply flawed. The apostle Paul's states that his source of instruction was from the Lord: "For we tell you this by the word of the Lord" (1 Thess 4:15). His source is drawn from the oral tradition of Jesus's eschatological discourse, which Paul used for his Thessalonian *church situation*. The parallels between Paul and Jesus are extensive, demonstrating that they have the same unified second coming in mind. If the Olivet Discourse was not intended for church instruction, then why would Paul use it as his main source for instructing the Thessalonian church? There are thirty parallels between Jesus's teaching on the second coming in the Olivet Discourse and Paul's teaching on the second coming in the Thessalonian letters. This comparison of Scripture with Scripture shows Paul's dependence on the Olivet Discourse tradition for teaching the Thessalonian church.

Table 4.
Jesus and Paul's Teachings

Matt 24–25	The Second Coming	1, 2 Thess
24:3–4	Christ is the Source	I.4:15
24:3, 27, 37, 39	Context: The Parousia	I.4:15, II.2:1, 8
24:4–5, 23–26	Do Not Be Deceived	II.2:3
24:6	Alarmed the End Has Come	II.2:2

the linguistic cohesion of Jesus's discourse and results in creating two separate Parousia events. The argumentation in Part 2 demonstrates rather the coherence of the Parousia event as a single, extended event.

24:15	The Antichrist's Desolation	II.2.4
24:21–22	Opposition by the Antichrist	II.2:3–4, 8–9
24:24	Deceiving Signs and Wonders	II.2:9–10
24:24	Elect Will Not Be Deceived	II.2:9–14
24:12	Lawlessness	II.2:3, 12
24:10–11	Apostasy of Many	II.2:3
24:13, 22, 31, 40–41 (Lk 21:28)	Surviving Believers Delivered	I.4:15, 17, 5:9, II.1:7
24:22, 29–31	Persecution Cut Short	II.1:6–7, 2:8
24:27, 30	Initiation of the Parousia	I.4:15, II.2:1, 8
24:29–30	Parousia Follows the Antichrist	II.2:8
24:27–30	Universal Perception	I.4:16, II.1:7–8
24:30	Jesus with Clouds	I.4:17
24:30	Power and Glory	II.1:9
24:31	Angelic Presence	I.4:16, II.1:7

24:31	Trumpet Call	I.4:16
24:31	Gathering	I.4:17, II.2:1
25:6	Meeting (*Apantēsis*)	I.4:17
24:37–41 (Lk 17:22–35)	Back-to-Back Rapture and Wrath	II.1:6–10
24:37–41	"Peace and Safety"	I.5:3
24:43	Thief in the Night	I.5:2, 4
24:37–41 (Lk 21:34)	Sudden Destruction for the Ungodly	I.5:2–3
24:29–30, 37–39	Initiation of the Day of the Lord	I.5:1–3, II.1:7–8
25:10–13 (Lk 21:36)	Inescapable for the Unprepared	I.5:3
24:32–33	Knowing the Season	I.5:1
24:45–46	The Faithful at His Coming	I.5:4–5, 8
24:42–25:13 (Lk 21:34–36)	Be Watchful and Expectant	I.5:6–8

This table illustrates that Jesus's and Paul's teaching on the second coming complement each other, portraying a consistent picture. The overwhelming parallels between the two support that they are clearly speaking of the same unified second coming of our Lord.

Some may object that there are elements "missing" in either Jesus's or Paul's teaching, which invalidates this comparison. For example, it may be argued that Paul never mentions the celestial disturbances found in Jesus's account, and therefore, Paul cannot be speaking about the same coming that Jesus teaches. This type of argumentation is unreasonable, demanding that when a New Testament writer teaches on a doctrine, he must be exhaustive in every element of it. Incidentally, Paul *does* refer to the celestial-disturbance event indirectly. In 1 Thess 5:3, he writes, "Sudden destruction comes on them, like labor pains on a pregnant woman, and they will surely not escape." Paul is drawing from Isa 13:6–10, which is a prominent Old Testament celestial-disturbance passage that Paul certainly had in mind.

Another objection pretribulationists make is noting that a "multitude" of angels is lacking in Paul's rapture passage in 1 Thess 4:13–18. Paul mentions only an archangel, while Jesus refers to a multitude of angels. This is selective with the evidence because we need to include Paul's entire Thessalonian teaching on Christ's coming. In his second Thessalonian epistle, he taught that Jesus will give relief to his persecuted church when "angels" (plural) accompany him at his return: "and to you who are being afflicted to give rest together with us when the Lord Jesus is revealed from heaven with his mighty angels" (2 Thess 1:7). We also know from Luke 9:26 that a host of angels will accompany Christ when he comes back for his church: "For whoever is ashamed of me and my words, the Son of Man will be ashamed of that person when he comes in his glory and in the glory of the Father and of the holy angels." These two accounts are compatible and complementary.

Finally, it may be objected that in Matt 24, angels do the gathering, while in Paul's teaching the Lord himself gathers. But this is not a contradiction since Paul never states that the Lord himself gathers. The verb in 1 Thess 4:17 "will be suddenly caught up" (*harpagēsometha*) is in the passive voice, with an *unstated* subject doing the action. Believers will meet the Lord in the sky, but the agent who gathers them is left unstated. It is reading into the text to assume that the Lord himself is the primary agent who does the gathering. Moreover, even if the text had said that Jesus gathered believers to himself, it would not rule out angels being used as his instrument to do so. For example, the Bible speaks about the Lord pouring out his wrath when he comes back (e.g. Rev 6:16–17), yet we know that Jesus will use angels as the instruments to execute his judgments (e.g. Matt 13:41, 2 Thess 1:7, Rev 8–9, Rev 14:15–19, Rev 15–16).

Pretribulationists are also inconsistent when applying their reasoning. They would never reason this way, for example, with John 14, which they rightly believe is a rapture passage. But John 14 is missing rapture elements that Paul includes in 1 Thess 4 (e.g. "a shout of command," "the voice of the archangel," "the trumpet of God.") Yet, despite these missing elements, pretribulationists would not conclude that John 14 is not a rapture passage. So why draw this conclusion about Matt 24, which contains many more elements from Paul's Thessalonian passage than are found in John 14? This interpretive approach is highly selective and biased. Furthermore, pretribulationists would never be this unreasonable with other doctrines containing this many parallels. What if this standard was applied to doctrines such as the deity of Christ or salvation? If every passage on a doctrinal topic required virtually the same elements as every other passage (as they require of rapture passages), we could never draw any conclusions. Imagine if we applied this standard to the Gospels. There would be no reason to possess four Gospel accounts because we would only need one. God ordained four portraits of the life of Jesus, with each Gospel writer giving additional elements that complement the others (e.g. genealogies, the birth of Jesus, the Lord's prayer, the

Gadarene demoniacs, the crucifixion, the resurrection, and so forth). It is correct to view Jesus's and Paul's teaching on the second coming, not as incompatible, but as complementary and harmonious.

Besides the apostle Paul, the Lord's eschatological discourse concerning his Parousia was utilized by James, Peter, and John, as well as other early Christian literature such as the Didache, all for their own respective *church teachings* (Jas 5:7–8, 2 Pet 3:4, 12, 1 John 2:28, Didache 16). The application of Jesus's Olivet Discourse by Paul and the other disciples for the nascent Christian church invalidates the pretribulation claim that the Olivet Discourse does not have the church in view. It is profoundly mistaken to dismiss Jesus's warnings in the Olivet Discourse for the church today, making them applicable to "tribulation saints."

In summary of this first contrast, it is a false dichotomy to disconnect the rapture from the unified extended event of the second coming. The second coming event includes the rapture when Christ comes for the last generation of church saints.[12]

---

12. Pretribulation interpreter Glenn R. Kreider is one of the very few exceptions within pretribulationism that uses the term *second coming* to encompass the rapture. The rapture, Kreider writes, is "an event prior to the tribulation, which *is* the second coming but is not the entire second coming. . . . In short, the rapture is the first stage or phase of the second coming. The rapture and second coming are not two separate events. They are two stages of one event. The first stage of the second coming, the rapture, occurs without warning and without signs. The second stage occurs seven years later" ("Rapture and the Day of the Lord," 83, emphasis his). His conception, however, is incoherent and even contradictory because his language indicates that he continues to maintain the pretribulation notion of the rapture and the second coming as two separate events disconnected by seven years. In other words, he separates these two events while claiming they "are not two separate events." He fails to use precise language explaining the New Testament usage of *parousia*. The rapture is never disconnected from the Parousia. In every New Testament usage of *parousia*, there is no indication that it is preceded by the day of the Lord. In Chapter 7, we will see clearly that the New Testament

Table 5.
Second Contrast

The Rapture Coming	The Second Coming
Jesus comes in the air	Jesus comes to the earth

Most of the critique above also applies to this next pretribulation contrast.[13] But this next one requires its own response. The Parousia/second coming of Christ begins in the air. We know this to be the case because Paul teaches that it will begin in the air and not on earth:

> For we tell you this by the word of the Lord, that we who are alive, who are left until the coming [*parousia*] of the Lord, will surely not go ahead of those who have fallen asleep. For the Lord himself will come down from heaven with a shout of command, with the voice of the archangel, and with the trumpet of God, and the dead in Christ will rise first. Then we who are alive, who are left, will be suddenly caught up together with them *in the clouds to meet the Lord in the air*. And so we will always be with the Lord. (1 Thess 4:15–17, cf. 2 Thess 1:4–10)

Similarly, Jesus teaches that his Parousia will begin when he returns in the clouds:

> For just like the lightning comes from the east and flashes to the west, so the coming [*parousia*] of the Son of Man will be. Wherever the corpse is, there the vultures will

writers denoted the *parousia* and the *day of the Lord* as coreferential. Incidentally, in his very next statement, Kreider reveals what may be motivating his interpretation: "One event in two stages *preserves both the doctrine of imminency* and the chronology of events seen in the Olivet Discourse" ("Rapture and the Day of the Lord," 83, emphasis mine). Unfortunately, this results in an incoherent interpretation that maintains his preconceived theological belief.

13. E.g. Feinberg argues for this next pretribulation contrast (*Case for the Pretribulation Rapture Position*, 81, cf. Walvoord, *Rapture Question*, 2nd ed., 93).

> gather. Immediately after the suffering of those days, the sun will be darkened, and the moon will not give its light; the stars will fall from heaven, and the powers of heaven will be shaken. Then the sign of the Son of Man *will appear in heaven*, and all the tribes of the earth will mourn. They will see the Son of Man *arriving on the clouds* of heaven with power and great glory. And he will send his angels with a loud trumpet blast, and they will gather his elect from the four winds, from one end of heaven to the other. (Matt 24:27–31)

> Then they will see the Son of Man *arriving in a cloud* with power and great glory. But when these things begin to happen, stand up and raise your heads, because your redemption is drawing near. (Luke 21:27–28)

Two similar passages should be mentioned from John's visions recorded in the book of Revelation, where (again) Jesus appears *in the sky* at his return *for a gathering*:

> Then I looked, and *a white cloud appeared, and seated on the cloud was one like a son of man*! He had a golden crown on his head and a sharp sickle in his hand. Then another angel came out of the temple, shouting in a loud voice to *the one seated on the cloud,* 'Use your sickle and start to reap, because the time to reap has come, since the earth's harvest is ripe!' So *the one seated on the cloud* swung his sickle over the earth, and the earth was reaped. (Rev 14:14–16, cf. Rev 1:7)

> The *sky* was split apart like a scroll being rolled up. . . . They said to the mountains and to the rocks, "Fall on us and hide us *from the face of the one who is seated on the throne and from the wrath of the Lamb,*" . . . . After these things I looked, and here was an enormous crowd that no one could count, made up of persons from every nation, tribe, people, and language, standing before the throne and before the Lamb dressed in long white robes, and with palm branches in their hands. . . . . Then one of the elders asked

> me, "These dressed in long white robes—who are they and where have they come from?" So I said to him, "My lord, you know the answer." Then he said to me, "These are the ones who have come out of the great tribulation. They have washed their robes and made them white in the blood of the Lamb!" (Rev 6:14, 16, 7:9, 13–14)

What these latter passages have in common, other than Christ appearing in the sky, is they depict the result of the rapture of the gathered saints.

A question remains concerning where believers go after they are united with Christ in the sky. Do they remain in the air? Do they go straight to heaven forever? Do they immediately descend to the earth?[14] Or is there another answer? The abode of the bride is said to be the New Jerusalem (Rev 21:9–10), which will descend and establish itself on earth (cf. Rev 21:1—22:5). But where will the people of God dwell between the time of the rapture and the descent of the New Jerusalem on earth? Four biblical passages picture the Lord escorting his people to heaven before the Father's presence. First, Paul wrote, "We do so because we know that the one who raised up Jesus will also raise us up with Jesus and will bring us with you into his [the Father's] presence" (2 Cor 4:14). Second, before his departure Jesus promised, "There are many dwelling places in my Father's house. Otherwise, I would have told you, because I am going away to make ready a place for you. And if I go and make ready a place for you, I will come again and take you to be with me, so that where I am you may be too" (John 14:2–3).[15] Third, the

14. Contra posttribulationism, Christ does not directly descend to earth immediately after the rapture (see Cosby, "Hellenistic Formal Receptions," 15–34).

15. The statement, "And if I go and make ready a place for you, I will come again," most certainly refers to the interadvent period between Jesus's ascension into heaven a few weeks later and when he returns for his people at his Parousia. Cf. Snow, "Israel, the Church, and the Last Half of Daniel's 70th Week," 13–14.

book of Revelation portrays: "Then one of the elders asked me, 'These dressed in long white robes—who are they and where have they come from?' So I said to him, 'My lord, you know the answer.' Then he said to me, 'These are the ones who have come out of the great tribulation. They have washed their robes and made them white in the blood of the Lamb! For this reason, they are before the throne of God, and they serve him day and night in his temple, and the one seated on the throne will shelter them'" (Rev 7:13–15). Fourth, the prophet Isaiah reads: "Your dead will come back to life; your corpses will rise up. Wake up and shout joyfully, you who live in the ground! For you will grow like plants drenched with the morning dew, and the earth will bring forth its dead spirits. Go, my people! Enter your inner rooms! Close your doors behind you! Hide for a little while, until his angry judgment is over. For look, the LORD is coming out of the place where he lives, to punish the sin of those who live on the earth. The earth will display the blood shed on it; it will no longer cover up its slain" (Isa 26:19–21). We learn from Isaiah the following sequence of events: first, the resurrection takes place; second, God's people are taken to the "inner rooms" to be protected; and third, the Lord comes out of his place to punish the wicked during the eschatological wrath.

These four passages picture Jesus escorting glorified believers into the presence of the Father after their resurrection and the rapture. While God's saints are protected in heaven, the Lord will mete out his eschatological day of the Lord's wrath via angels. God's people to be sure will not remain in heaven; after God's wrath, the New Jerusalem will descend to the earth for the millennium and eternity.[16]

16. There is debate on the question of whether the New Jerusalem descends at the beginning or end of the millennium; but for my point here, the timing of that event is not relevant. The biblical evidence supports that God's people are ushered into heaven after the resurrection and the rapture.

The second coming, therefore, begins at an earlier point before Jesus *physically* returns to earth to set up this world as his kingdom (Rev 11:15). The main events can only be summarized here: (1) After Jesus ushers God's saints before the throne of the Father in heaven, he will direct the trumpet judgments through his angels.[17] Jesus's Parousia judgments will fulfill his righteous purposes for the wicked. (2) As Davidic king, Jesus will physically return to earth to lead Jewish remnants back to Israel as they recognize him as their long-awaited messiah, fulfilling Daniel's seventy weeks prophecy. (3) The final series of God's wrath are then executed through the bowls. (4) The nations' armies and kings will encamp at Armageddon, planning to attack the newly-coronated Christ: "Then I saw the beast and the kings of the earth and their armies assembled to do battle with the one who rode the horse and with his army" (Rev 19:19). Jesus will retrieve his heavenly armies and preemptively attack the beasts, kings, and the armies of the earth, vanquishing them. (5) The millennial period eventually ensues shortly afterwards.[18]

In summary, it is a mistake to disconnect the rapture from the Parousia. The second coming/Parousia begins in the sky when Jesus returns to the clouds to resurrect and rapture the saints of God. The second coming continues to unfold with a manifold of divine purposes, including Jesus eventually arriving physically on earth to deliver a remnant of Israel, retrieve his heavenly army to go to battle, and to rule during the millennium.

17. Incidentally, the reference in Rev 19:13 of Jesus's robe being "dipped in blood" likely indicates his involvement in judging his enemies through the series of trumpet and bowl judgments.

18. See the following commentary on Jesus's physical itinerary: Van Kampen, *The Sign*, 365–464; Snow, *The Passover King*.

Table 6.
Third Contrast

The Rapture Coming	**The Second Coming**
No signs – imminent	Signs – not imminent

This third contrast is especially important for pretribulationists, who believe that there are no signs for the church to look for before the rapture.[19] Most significantly, they deny that the Antichrist's great tribulation will happen before the rapture. Signs, they argue, are for "tribulation saints." The contrast in Table 6 is a key criterion for interpreting prophetic passages from a pretribulation perspective.[20] For example, Wayne Brindle adduces the following principle for determing imminence: "The passage speaks of Christ's return as at any moment."[21] This is circular reasoning. Brindle begins with his conclusion, then uses it as evidence for his conclusion. In essence, this reasons that a passage is about the rapture if events *aren't* mentioned before it, while a passage is about the second coming if events *are* mentioned before it. This is an all-too-common practice for how pretribulation interpreters argue for imminence. Imminence as a theological axiom is ingrained so deeply that they do not seem to be aware of this circular reasoning. It is selective evidence that excludes any passage as a rapture passage that mentions signs or events. If pretribulation interpreters want to begin with an unbiased principle, they should consider all passages *regardless* of whether they mention signs. For example, Mark 13:28–29 speaks of Christ's return as near, but it also mentions signs that must precede his coming: "Learn this parable from the

19. E.g. Feinberg, *Case for the Pretribulation Rapture Position*, 80–81.

20. Feinberg, "Response," 157–58.

21. Brindle, "Biblical Evidence," 139.

fig tree: Whenever its branch becomes tender and puts out its leaves, you know that summer is near. So also you, when you see these things happening, know that he is near, right at the door." Jesus predicted that summer will arrive only after the intervening events of branches become "tender" and put out "leaves." This text is from Jesus's eschatological Discourse, but since it mentions signs, pretribulation interpreters exclude it out of hand. This interpretive method begins with a stacked deck, *creating a theory that is impossible to be falsified.* Whether you discuss physics, philosophy, history, or theology, if your theory does not allow the possibility of being falsifiable with counter evidence, then the theory is invalid. This approach makes it impossible for contrary evidence to exist. Just so I am not misunderstood, for a theory to be falsifiable, it does not mean that it is necessarily false—it could be true. It means that a valid theory requires objective criteria that would allow it to be falsified *if there were evidence against it.* One of the most common red flags of an unfalsifiable theory is circular reasoning. In our case, the pretribulation hermeneutic operates from a preconceived theological idea that determines the outcome for imminence in advance.

Interpretive criteria, therefore, should allow for the widest range of evidence, lest it be prejudicial. The criteria should not be crafted so narrowly as to exclude biblical evidence that might contradict one's theological system. The fundamental flaw of circular reasoning makes this pretribulation contrast invalid as a sound hermeneutic principle.

Table 7.
Fourth Contrast

The Rapture Coming	**The Second Coming**
Only his own see him	Every eye will see him

Our final pretribulation contrast does not work either.[22] When Jesus returns, he is not returning secretly, incognito, so that only Christians will see his glorious manifestation.[23] This will not be like his first coming, which was localized to the vicinity of Bethlehem. Instead, he is coming back in *power and glory* for the entire world to see him. After the rapture, the world will not be looking around scratching their heads, wondering what just happened. This would make Jesus's return out to be an anti-climactic, *un*glorious event. It will not be a "dog whistle" return that only believers are able to hear and see. That may work for fantasy novels, but it is not biblical reality. When Jesus comes back for his saints, his Parousia will be loud and visible! "For the Lord himself will come down from heaven with a *shout of command, with the voice of the archangel, and with the trumpet of God*, and the dead in Christ will rise first" (1 Thess 4:16, cf. Matt 24:30–31). The return of Christ will be glorious, because while the world is hating and putting to death God's saints, the Great Rescuer will blast through the sky and deliver them! The Lord then will pour out his wrath upon this wicked world. That is a glorious return.

It may be objected that since the apostle Paul taught that Jesus will come back as a thief, this indicates a secret rapture: "For you know quite well that the day of the Lord will come in the same way as a thief in the night" (1 Thess 5:2). There are two problems with this. First, in 1 Thess 5, Paul uses the thief simile to indicate the element of *suddenness* with respect to those who lack watchfulness. "Now when

22. To be sure, not all pretribulation interpreters believe that the rapture will occur in secret.

23. Contra Hitchcock, *Could the Rapture Happen Today?*, 80. See also Thomas Ice's article "Differences Between the Rapture and the Second Coming" (https://www.pre-trib.org/other-articles-by-dr-thomas-ice/message/differences-between-the-rapture-and-the-second-coming).

they are saying, 'There is peace and security,' then sudden destruction comes on them, like labor pains on a pregnant woman, and they will surely not escape" (1 Thess 5:3, cf. 2 Thess 1:1–12). His metaphor does not mean *stealthiness*, as if Christ will come back undetectably. Rather, his return will come upon the wicked suddenly because they are unprepared. When this happens, the ungodly are not going to look around, wondering if UFOs just beamed up millions of persons. Second, Paul teaches that while Christ's return will be like a thief for unbelievers, it will not be like a thief for believers: "But you, brothers and sisters, are not in the darkness for the day to overtake you like a thief would. For you all are sons of the light and sons of the day. We are not of the night nor of the darkness" (1 Thess 5:4–5, cf. vv. 6–14). Incidentally, within his discourse, Jesus places his thief-return *after* the great tribulation (see Matt 24:43).

It is Jesus's universal visibility that is really the focus of such passages. Here are some other passages that convey the universal visibility of Jesus's return:

> Immediately after the suffering of those days, the sun will be darkened, and the moon will not give its light; the stars will fall from heaven, and the powers of heaven will be shaken. *Then the sign of the Son of Man will appear in heaven, and all the tribes of the earth will mourn. They will see the Son of Man arriving on the clouds of heaven with power and great glory* (Matt 24:29–30).

> And there will be signs in the sun and moon and stars, and on the earth nations will be in distress, anxious over the roaring of the sea and the surging waves. *People will be fainting from fear and from the expectation of what is coming on the world, for the powers of the heavens will be shaken. Then they will see the Son of Man arriving in a cloud with power and great glory*. But when these things begin to happen, stand up and raise your heads, because your redemption is drawing near (Luke 21:25–28).

> Look! He is returning with the clouds, and *every eye will see him*, even those who pierced him, and all the tribes on the earth will mourn because of him. This will certainly come to pass! Amen (Rev 1:7).

> Then I looked when the Lamb opened the sixth seal, and a huge earthquake took place; the sun became as black as sackcloth made of hair, and the full moon became blood red; and the stars in the sky fell to the earth like a fig tree dropping its unripe figs when shaken by a fierce wind. *The sky was split apart like a scroll being rolled up*, and every mountain and island was moved from its place. Then the kings of the earth, the very important people, the generals, the rich, the powerful, and everyone, slave and free, hid themselves in the caves and among the rocks of the mountains. *They said to the mountains and to the rocks, "Fall on us and hide us from the face of the one who is seated on the throne and from the wrath of the Lamb*, because the great day of their wrath has come, and who is able to withstand it?" (Rev 6:12–17).

These passages picture, not only believers, but unbelievers recognizing the presence of Christ's return. It will be universal in scope—a time when Jesus is glorified through his actions of deliverance *and* judgment. Everyone alive at the time will undoubtedly witness his *par excellence* theophany.

For these reasons, it is an artificial distinction that only believers will discern Jesus's return. Unlike his first coming, Jesus will display his glory so that every eye will see him when he returns to deliver his saints and mete out his wrath.

Conclusion

This chapter examined the Parousia presupposition that disconnects the rapture from the second coming/Parousia. This dichotomy is foundational to the pretribulation interpretive framework. I began critiquing this presupposition using a comparative illustration from the Gospels. Then I critiqued four common pretribulation contrasts that purport to teach an interval between the rapture and the second coming. It was concluded that these contrasts are artificial, lacking biblical support. The rapture instead belongs to the larger unified event of the second coming. In Chapter 6, I will continue to build on my critique of the Parousia presupposition by demonstrating that the second coming does not begin with the battle of Armageddon as is commonly believed.

Chapter 6

THE SECOND COMING DOES NOT BEGIN WITH ARMAGEDDON

Pretribulationists believe that the second coming begins with the battle of Armageddon.[1] This belief is so deep-seated that it is never challenged. I have already discussed that Paul teaches that the Parousia will start with the resurrection and rapture: "But each in his own order: Christ, the firstfruits; then *when Christ comes* [*parousia*], those who belong to him" (1 Cor 15:23, cf. 15:50–55). The souls of the saints who have died will come with Christ to receive their new bodies: "For if we believe that Jesus died and rose again, so also we believe that *God will bring with him those who have fallen asleep as Christians*. For we tell you this by the word of the Lord, that we who are alive, who are left *until the coming* [*parousia*] of the Lord, will surely not go ahead of those who have fallen asleep" (1 Thess 4:14–15). Saints who are alive at this time will be raptured together with the newly resurrected: "Then we who are alive, who are left, will be suddenly *caught up together with*

1. Feinberg, *Case for the Pretribulation Rapture Position*, 81; Pentecost, *Things to Come*, 340; Walvoord, *The Rapture Question*, 2nd ed., 62. Posttribulationism believes the same; e.g. Gundry, *Church and the Tribulation*, 83–84, 90–92.

them in the clouds to meet the Lord in the air. And so we will always be with the Lord" (1 Thess 4:17). The Parousia begins as a deliverance event, whereas the battle of Armageddon is a later development of the Parousia that will complete the day of the Lord's wrath after the trumpet and bowl judgments.

This chapter continues to critique the Parousia presupposition with another line of evidence. I will elaborate more why the second coming does not start with the battle of Armageddon. First, I will begin by contrasting significant dissimilarities between Matt 24:29–31 and Rev 19. Second, and the focus of this chapter, I will examine three key events associated with the second coming that occur at an earlier point before Armageddon takes place: (1) the resurrection of the saints, (2) the beginning of the day of the Lord's wrath, and (3) the inauguration of Christ's physical kingdom. Because these events occur before the battle of Armageddon, the establishment of the second coming will not begin with Armageddon. Certainly, the battle of Armageddon *belongs* to the unified extended event of the second coming, but it will be shown that the second coming of Jesus will began at an earlier point.

Matthew 24:29–31 Is Not Describing the Battle of Armageddon

Revelation 19:11 is commonly cited as evidence that the battle of Armageddon begins at the second coming: "Then I saw heaven opened and here came a white horse! The one riding it was called 'Faithful' and 'True,' and with justice he judges and goes to war." The context, however, does not reflect this. Revelation 19:11–21 is often linked with the classic second coming passage in Matt 24:29–31. However, the only element common to both passages is the depiction of Jesus coming from "heaven." In Matt 24:29–31 (cf. Luke 21:25–28), the message is that the sign of the Son of Man is appearing for *global deliverance of the saints*. In Rev 19:11–21, there is no gathering event of the saints, which would certainly be expected if this were the beginning of the second coming. The picture, instead, is of Christ appearing for *local judgment* of the Armageddon battlefield. In addition, in Matt 24:29–31, the Son of Man comes down to the sky, arriving on the clouds *to gather the saints*. In Rev 19:11–21, Christ comes *to destroy* the armies of the nations.[2] Most importantly, in Matt 24:29–31, the return of Jesus is followed by parables and similitudes that illustrate the *beginning* of God's wrath. In Rev 19, the battle of Armageddon depicts the *completion* of God's wrath, occurring after the trumpet and bowl judgments.

These incompatible aspects signal two different settings. But my main point in this chapter does not rely solely on these observations. Instead, this chapter will focus on three important events associated with the second coming that will occur at an earlier point before Armageddon takes place.

Matthew 24:30 is Not Armageddon

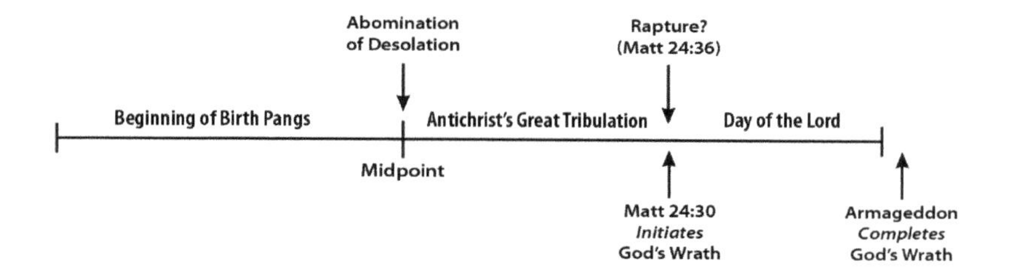

The Resurrection Occurs Before Armageddon

In this first line of evidence, I will argue that the resurrection

2. The mention of Christ coming on *clouds* is showcased in significant passages depicting Christ's return, e.g. Luke 21:27, 1 Thess 4:17, and Rev 14:14–16. Some interpreters may dismiss this point as unimportant, but it is odd that this key theophanic element of clouds would be missing from Rev 19:11–21 if this were supposed to be the main second coming passage.

of the saints will not occur in conjunction with the battle of Armageddon. Pretribulationists place the resurrection of Old Testament saints and "tribulation saints" at the time of Armageddon. In the pretribulation framework, the resurrection of church saints occurs seven years earlier.[3] I will defend, instead, that there is no resurrection taking place at the time of Armageddon. The evidence for a resurrection at this time is often drawn from Rev 20:4–5:

> (4) Then I saw thrones, and they sat on them, and judgment was given to them. And I saw the souls of those who had been beheaded because of their testimony of Jesus and because of the word of God, and those who had not worshiped the beast or his image, and had not received the mark on their forehead and on their hand; and *they came to life* and reigned with Christ for a thousand years. (5) The rest of the dead did not come to life until the thousand years were completed. This is the first resurrection (Rev 20:4–5 NASB).

There is debate among commentators whether v. 4 denotes one, two, or even three groups; for our purposes, the question is whether those "beheaded" and those who "came to life" are two separate groups. In the book of Revelation, it is difficult to avoid the close connection between those who refuse to worship the beast and those who are martyred (e.g. Rev 13:15–16). For this main reason, we should understand the beheaded mentioned in v. 4 as those who came to life.[4] Another related issue concerns the meaning of "they came to life" (*ezēsan*). Interpreters commonly construe this in temporal terms. It is better, however, to see this as a description of their resurrected *state*, something they previously experienced as portrayed earlier in the narrative (cf. Rev 7:9–17). For the

3. Pentecost, *Things to Come*, 410–11.

4. See Mathewson, *Revelation*, 274–76. To be sure, this does not require that the beheaded are the only saints who came to life, since they are likely being viewed as part of the larger people of God (cf. Rev 7:9–17).

following reasons, the statement "they came to life" is not a chronological or temporal indication that a resurrection is taking place at this point in Rev 20:4–5.

First, the activity of "coming life" is not giving the chronological timing of the resurrection because it links back to the resurrection event vividly portrayed earlier in Rev 7:9–17 (cf. Rev 14:14–16, 15:2–4). In Rev 7:9–17, just before God's wrath begins, the saints receive their *reward of resurrection*; while in Rev 20:4, after God's wrath, the saints receive their *reward to rule* with Christ in his kingdom (Rev 2:26, 3:21). In Rev 20:4, John is invoking previous imagery of the beheaded souls and the cause for their martyrdom: "for their testimony to Jesus and for the word of God. They had not worshiped the beast or its image and had not received its mark on their foreheads or their hands" (cf. Rev 13:15–16). In the fifth seal vision, John links their martyrdom with their former disembodied status as souls under the altar:

> Now when the Lamb opened the fifth seal, I saw under the altar the souls of those who had been violently killed because of the word of God and because of the testimony they had given. They cried out with a loud voice, "How long, Sovereign Master, holy and true, before you judge those who live on the earth and avenge our blood?" Each of them was given a long white robe and they were told to rest for a little longer, until the full number was reached of both their fellow servants and their brothers who were going to be killed just as they had been (Rev 6:9–11).

Soon after this promise is given, these saints are seen standing before the throne and holding in their hands palm branches, which signifies resurrection: "After these things I looked, and here was an enormous crowd that no one could count, made up of persons from every nation, tribe, people, and language, standing before the throne and before the Lamb dressed in long white robes, and with palm branches in their hands" (Rev 7:9).

Second, the armies of heaven (Rev 19:14) who accompany Christ into battle are shown to already possess glorified, resurrected bodies and are described as redeemed saints. Revelation 17:14 associates these redeemed saints with the armies of heaven in 19:14 that accompany and follow Christ into the eschatological battle:

> [The beast and kings] will make war with the Lamb, but the Lamb will conquer them, because he is Lord of lords and King of kings, and those accompanying the Lamb are the called, chosen, and faithful (Rev 17:14).

> The armies that are in heaven, dressed in white, clean, fine linen, *were following him* on white horses (Rev 19:14).

Revelation 17:14 most certainly anticipates the battle depicted in ch. 19. I say "anticipates" because the aftermath is portrayed in Rev 19:11—20:3. The activity of "accompanying" is linked with the ones who are "called, chosen, and faithful," which indicates that these are redeemed saints. In addition, the attire of the redeemed saints in 19:7–8 is described identically as the attire of the armies of heaven in 19:14:

> Let us rejoice and exult and give him glory, because the wedding celebration of the Lamb has come, and his bride has made herself ready. She was permitted to be *dressed in bright, clean, fine linen (for the fine linen is the righteous deeds of the saints)* (Rev 19:7–8).

> The armies that are in heaven, *dressed in white, clean, fine linen*, were following him on white horses (Rev 19:14).

This language parallels the most explicit resurrection passage in the Old Testament:

> "Many of those who sleep in the dusty ground will awake—some to everlasting life, and others to shame and everlasting abhorrence. But the wise will *shine like the brightness* of the heavenly expanse. And those bringing many to righteousness will be like the stars forever and ever. . . . Many will be

> *purified, made clean, and refined*, but the wicked will go on being wicked. None of the wicked will understand, though the wise will understand" (Dan 12:2–3, 10, cf. Dan 11:35).

Third, the saints coming with Christ from heaven in Rev 19 are portrayed as already having been resurrected, while the saints coming with Christ from heaven in 1 Thess 4:14–16 are disembodied, non-resurrected saints:

> For if we believe that Jesus died and rose again, so also we believe that God *will bring with him those* [i.e. the disembodied saints] who have fallen asleep as Christians. For we tell you this by the word of the Lord, that we who are alive, who are left until the coming of the Lord, will surely not go ahead of those who have fallen asleep. For the Lord himself will come down from heaven with a shout of command, with the voice of the archangel, and with the trumpet of God, *and the dead in Christ will rise first* (1 Thess 4:14–16).

Paul's resurrection teaching in 1 Thess 4:14–18 describes an event that will occur at an earlier period than what is being described in Rev 19–20.

For these reasons, the timing of the resurrection should be viewed as having taken place in 7:9–17 and not in conjunction with Armageddon. The motif in the book of Revelation is becoming an overcomer against the Beast's system. In Rev 20:4, John is thematically contrasting the state of the victory of the resurrected martyrs with the state of the defeat of the enemies of God. He is not narrating the timing of the resurrection in 20:4 as a result of Armageddon. Rather, when he says "they came alive," he is drawing attention to their prominent *status*. They are viewed as already having been resurrected, which took place between the sixth and seventh seals, while Rev 19 views them as those who make up the armies of heaven following Christ into battle. At that time, they are given their reward to sit on thrones and co-reign with Christ over the conquered nations in his kingdom.[5]

5. On this latter point, see Kurschner, *Linguistic Approach to*

The Day of the Lord's Wrath Begins Before Armageddon

The second reason the second coming does not begin at the time of Armageddon concerns the start of the day of the Lord's wrath. No one disagrees that the battle of Armageddon belongs to God's eschatological wrath. It is important, however, to recognize that Armageddon *concludes* the day of the Lord's wrath. It does not begin it. The biblical writers connected the beginning of the second coming with the onset of the day of the Lord's wrath. The same day the rapture will occur will be the same day that the Lord's wrath begins. In Chapter 7, I will argue there is no gap between the rapture and God's wrath; it will occur back to back.

In this section, I will explain why God's wrath, which is associated with the second coming, will occur before the battle of Armageddon. The apostle Paul links the return of Christ to the day of the Lord's wrath (1 Thess 4:13—5:9). As noted previously, Paul teaches that when Christ returns to pour out his wrath, his return will be like a thief, occurring suddenly like a woman in labor: "For you know quite well that the day of the Lord will come in the same way as a thief in the night. Now when they are saying, 'There is peace and security,' then sudden destruction comes on them, like labor pains on a pregnant woman, and they will surely not escape" (1 Thess 5:2–3). In his Olivet Discourse, Jesus also taught that the first day of his Parousia will begin with destruction. To reinforce this point, Jesus used a cluster of vivid illustrations, including Noah and the flood, "one taken and one left," and the metaphors of the thief, the master of

---

Revelation 19:11—20:6; Kurschner and Svigel, "Who Sat on the Thrones in Revelation 20:4?" Incidentally, I do not want to rule out that angels *as well* will likely accompany Christ at Armageddon. Angels help administer the trumpet and bowl judgments, so there is nothing that requires this to be either/or. The plural "armies" may suggest both angels and God's redeemed.

the household, and the ten virgins (Matt 24:37—25:30, cf. Lot and Sodom in Luke 17:28–30). To note a couple of these:

> "Just as it was in the days of Noah, so too it will be in the days of the Son of Man. People were eating, they were drinking, they were marrying, they were being given in marriage—right up to the day Noah entered the ark. Then the flood came and destroyed them all. Likewise, just as it was in the days of Lot, people were eating, drinking, buying, selling, planting, building; but on the day Lot went out from Sodom, fire and sulfur rained down from heaven and destroyed them all. It will be the same on the day the Son of Man is revealed. On that day, anyone who is on the roof, with his goods in the house, must not come down to take them away, and likewise the person in the field must not turn back" (Luke 17:26–31).

> "For in those days before the flood, people were eating and drinking, marrying and giving in marriage, until the day Noah entered the ark. And they knew nothing until the flood came and took them all away. It will be the same at the coming of the Son of Man" (Matt 24:38–39).

These analogies clearly do not picture the battle of Armageddon because they emphasize the beginning of God's wrath, not its climax. Jesus teaches that before his second coming, the people of the world will be going on with their ordinary business, oblivious to impending divine judgment. How could people be going on with their ordinary business, unaware of God's wrath, during the trumpet and bowl judgments? Since the battle of Armageddon occurs after these judgments, the second coming cannot begin with Armageddon. This would remove the element of surprise, which is the whole point of invoking the thief metaphor in the first place. The resurrection and rapture will be followed by the eschatological wrath of God through the trumpet and bowl judgments, climaxing in the battle of Armageddon.[6] The apostle Paul, Jesus, and the book of Revelation teach that the day of the Lord will begin *suddenly*, like a thief. As in the days of Noah, the wicked "knew nothing until the flood came and took them all away." Peter also draws from the thief motif from Jesus's Olivet Discourse, illustrating the sudden destruction when the Parousia begins (see 2 Pet 3:10–12).

Armageddon, then, should not be considered the beginning of the second coming. If it is, the teaching of Jesus, Paul, and the book of Revelation become incoherent. By the time the battle begins, the unbelieving world will have already been pummeled by the devastating day-of-the-Lord trumpet and bowl judgments. How would Jesus's return at Armageddon catch the ungodly off guard? The sixth trumpet by itself results in one-third of humanity perishing (Rev 9:18). By then the wicked will certainly know that the trumpets and bowls are divine wrath and not some freakish, natural series of occurrences (see Rev 6:15–17, 8:13, 9:20–21, 11:3–13, 11:15, 11:18–19, 14:6–11, 15:5–6, 16:8–11, 16:21, 17:14, cf. Luke 21:25–28). When the kings and the armies of the world prepare for Armageddon and go after the one who has been the cause of their torment (cf. Rev 16:12–16, 17:12–14, 19:17–21), the world will have already been beleaguered by God's wrath. In short, the great battle climaxes God's eschatological wrath. It does not initiate it.

With this understanding, it makes sense why Jesus illustrates the great separation at the rapture (cf. Matt 24:31). The Antichrist's great tribulation begins at the midpoint of the seven-year period. At that time, the world will be saying "peace and safety," as they think they are secure under the Antichrist's system. Being oblivious of God's impending

6. More specifically, prewrath views the battle as occurring between the sixth and seventh bowl judgment (see Rev 16:16–17). For practical purposes, however, I have stated that the battle culminates the day of the Lord's wrath.

judgment, at an unknown hour or day (Matt 24:36), the days of great tribulation will be cut short by Jesus's return beginning in the clouds. He will rapture his people, and on that same day, God's wrath will begin with the trumpet judgments, followed by the bowl judgments, and culminating in the great battle of Armageddon.

Those who have objected to understanding that the second coming/day of the Lord begins earlier than the battle of Armageddon often cite Rev 16:14–16 as evidence that it will begin at the time of Armageddon:[7]

> For they are the spirits of the demons performing signs who go out to the kings of the earth to bring them together for the battle that will take place on the great day of God, the All-Powerful. (Look! I will come like a thief! Blessed is the one who stays alert and does not lose his clothes so that he will not have to walk around naked and his shameful condition be seen.) Now the spirits gathered the kings and their armies to the place that is called Armageddon in Hebrew.

It is argued that since the future-tense statement "I will come like a thief" is in the context of the sixth bowl judgment and a reference to Armageddon, it means that Jesus will not return before Armageddon. This understanding, however, is misconstrued for several reasons. Just before the sixth bowl concludes, there is the editorial exhortation: "(Look! I will come like a thief! Blessed is the one who stays alert and does not lose his clothes so that he will not have to walk around naked and his shameful condition be seen)" (Rev 16:15). Amid this apocalyptic portrayal, God warns readers to be spiritually prepared to avoid his wrath. The book of Revelation warns us before (Rev 1:7), during (Rev 16:15), and after (Rev 22:12, 20) the narrative. The exhortation in Rev 16:15 is *parenthetical*, and as such, is not intended to give a temporal indicator as to when the Lord will return,

7. Gundry, *Church and the Tribulation*, 37.

as is often interpreted.[8] This exhortation, then, does not mean that Jesus's Parousia has not yet occurred and that the church is still on earth. The Parousia begins between the sixth seal and seventh seal, which is followed by the trumpet and bowl judgments. The sixth bowl prepares for the battle of Armageddon. As noted earlier, it makes no sense to say Jesus is coming back as a "thief" after the world has already been pummeled by his earth-destroying judgments. Translations such as the New English Translation correctly recognize this verse as an aside, thereby placing parentheses around the exhortation. In the study note, the New English Translation comments, "These lines are parenthetical, forming an aside to the narrative. The speaker here is the Lord Jesus Christ himself rather than the narrator."

How, then, should we understand why this parenthetical statement is placed at this point? The exhortation is immediately followed by the reference to the battle of Armageddon (v. 16). Since Armageddon occurs in the context of the completion of God's wrath, the most likely meaning for this association is that this climactic battle represents the extended day of the Lord's wrath. This common linguistic device is a *meronymy*, which means a part-whole relationship. For example, when we say "I see faces," the term *face* (being the most prominent feature of the body) represents the whole *person*. Similarly, the battle of Armageddon is the most prominent feature of all the elements within God's eschatological wrath. It is a mistake, then, to apply Rev 16:15 only to Armageddon and not to the entirety of the series of the trumpet and bowl judgments.

I need to make another comment on this verse. The meaning of "I will come like a thief!" is followed by a qualification: "one who stays alert and does not lose his clothes so that he will not have to walk around naked and

8. E.g. Mounce, *Revelation*, 300–301.

his shameful condition be seen" (cf. Rev 3:18). Some believe this refers to believers who lose their salvation because they lose their faith and are judged as unbelievers along with the rest of the wicked. The question of whether believers can lose their salvation is not going to be determined by this single verse. My theological conviction is that Scripture consistently teaches the perseverance of the saints. I take this warning, as I do with other similar warnings in the Bible, as a *means* by which God perseveres the faith of the saints by warning them to be spiritually vigilant. Likewise, in Rev 3:18, I take the warning to mean that the one who does not stay alert will be revealed as a false believer. These will find themselves on the receiving end of God's wrath. The thrust of the book of Revelation is on those who will have victory through enduring faith and overcoming the beast's persecution and deception. It does not entertain lukewarm Christians as victorious (Rev 3:16). In the parable of the ten virgins, there are only two groups: wise virgins and foolish virgins. All five wise virgins were spiritually alert when the bridegroom arrived (Matt 25:1–13). Jesus is going to refine the faith of his bride through the great tribulation so that he comes for a blameless people (cf. Rev 14:12, Dan 11:33–36, 12:10). The false believer is the one who will lose his clothes and walk around naked in a shameful condition. Being naked and in shame, therefore, exposes the person in the day of the Lord's wrath for who they are. Faith is the true mark of a believer. But those with a veneer of Christianity will find themselves thief-exposed amid the Lord's wrath.

The parenthetical warning within the narrative of this apocalyptic period teaches us that those who are not spiritually watchful for the Lord will find themselves experiencing these judgments. Hearing the book of Revelation read to them (Rev 1:3), John's original audience would have construed this warning, not as some clue to the timing of the Parousia, as some interpreters would think, but a warning against spiritual unwatchfulness, lest they experience the consequences of God's wrath. Those who are spiritually watchful for the Lord's return will find themselves fighting alongside the divine alliance: "[The kings of the world] will make war with the Lamb, but the Lamb will conquer them, because he is Lord of lords and King of kings, and those accompanying the Lamb are the called, chosen, and faithful" (Rev 17:14).

In summary, the day of the Lord's wrath will begin before the battle of Armageddon. The battle itself will be the climax of God's earthly judgment upon the wicked. And since God's eschatological wrath is associated with the second coming, it follows in this additional line of evidence that the second coming will occur before Armageddon.

God's Kingdom Begins Before the Battle of Armageddon

We turn to our third reason the second coming should not be understood as beginning with the battle of Armageddon.[9] Jesus's *physical* kingdom is associated with his second coming (e.g. Acts 1:6–7; Matt 6:10, 24:14, 26:29; 1 Cor 15:23–28). By definition, Jesus's rule on *earth* is the goal of his Parousia—i.e. his *presence*. As I will contend, the Bible portrays that Jesus will take possession of earth as his kingdom at an earlier point, before the battle of Armageddon. Since Jesus's physical kingdom is established on earth prior to the battle of Armageddon, it follows that his second coming begins before the battle, as well.

Immediately after the seventh trumpet pronouncement, we read, "The nations were enraged" (Rev 11:18). For evidence that the Parousia has already occurred by this point, we can look as far back as the eschatological Psalms. Among them is Psalm 110, which anticipates this battle *after* the beginning

9. Contra Feinberg, "Arguing for the Rapture," 198.

of the reclamation of Messiah's earthly kingdom:

> The LORD extends your *dominion* from Zion. *Rule* in the midst of your enemies. Your people willingly follow you when you go into battle. On the holy hills at sunrise the dew of your youth belongs to you. The LORD makes this promise on oath and will not revoke it: "You are an eternal priest after the pattern of Melchizedek." O Lord, at your right hand he strikes down kings in the day he unleashes his anger. He executes judgment against the nations. He fills the valleys with corpses; he shatters their heads over the vast battlefield. From the stream along the road he drinks; then he lifts up his head (Ps 110:2–7).

In addition, a good portion of the second Psalm prophesies of the future coronation of the Messiah, which will provoke the anger of the nations:

> Why do the nations rebel? Why are the countries devising plots that will fail? The kings of the earth form a united front; the rulers collaborate against the LORD and his anointed king. They say, "Let's tear off the shackles they've put on us. Let's free ourselves from their ropes." The one enthroned in heaven laughs in disgust; the Lord taunts them. Then he angrily speaks to them and terrifies them in his rage, saying, "I myself have installed my king on Zion, my holy hill." The king says, "I will announce the LORD's decree. He said to me: 'You are my son. This very day I have become your father. Ask me, and I will give you the nations as your inheritance, the ends of the earth as your personal property. You will break them with an iron scepter; you will smash them like a potter's jar.'" So now, you kings, do what is wise; you rulers of the earth, submit to correction. Serve the LORD in fear. Repent in terror. Give sincere homage. Otherwise he will be angry, and you will die because of your behavior, when his anger quickly ignites. How blessed are all who take shelter in him! (Ps 2:1–12).

The kingdom pronouncement at the seventh trumpet, with Christ reclaiming this world, *precipitates* the armies of the world to marshal a military campaign against him. He will strike them while they are gathered at Armageddon.[10] When Christ's Parousia begins, the elect are gathered (Rev 7:9–17) and the trumpet judgments begin to execute God's wrath. The final seventh trumpet pronounces the establishment of Christ's physical kingdom, which is followed by the bowl judgments of the final wrath of God, culminating in the battle of Armageddon. Incidentally, the immediate context of the battle gives this description: "Then I saw the beast and the kings of the earth and their armies assembled to do battle with the one who rode the horse and with his army" (Rev 19:19, cf. 16:12–16). This indicates that Jesus will have already returned before the battle. Why will the armies of the nations go through all that trouble to assemble and go to war *if there is no opponent in the first place*! The text reveals that they know whom they are going after: "to do battle with the one who rode the horse and with his army" (Rev 19:19).

For these reasons, Christ's earthly kingdom, which presupposes his Parousia (i.e. his presence) is announced at an earlier point before the battle of Armageddon takes place. It is mistaken to understand that the second coming begins with this event.

Conclusion

In this chapter, I continued to critique the Parousia presupposition, which disconnects the rapture from the second coming. Pretribulationists believe that these are two separate events intervened by the seven-year period. Scripture instead teaches that the two-fold event of the rapture/resurrection is the initial event of the second coming. The

10. Armageddon ("Mount of Megiddo") was a city on a hill by the name of Megiddo overlooking the Valley of Jezreel, also called the Valley of Megiddo. On the meaning of this term in the Bible (esp. Rev 16:16), see Kurschner, *Antichrist Before the Day of the Lord*, 259–61.

rapture belongs to the unified extended Parousia. I examined the pretribulation framework that places the start of the second coming with the battle of Armageddon. It was shown that three key eschatological events linked with the second coming will occur at a point *earlier* than Armageddon: (1) the resurrection of the saints, (2) the day of the Lord's wrath, and (3) the inauguration of Christ's physical kingdom at the seventh trumpet. In conclusion, the Parousia presupposition lacks biblical support. It cannot be maintained that the second coming begins with Armageddon. In the next chapter, I will round out my thesis with a final line of evidence for understanding that the rapture and the resurrection are the initial events of Christ's second coming. It will focus on demonstrating that there is no gap of time between the rapture and the second coming.

Chapter 7

THE SECOND COMING BEGINS WITH THE RAPTURE

I will summarize the lines of critique up to this point concerning the Parousia presupposition. In Chapter 4, I described key terms that the New Testament authors used to describe the unified extended event of the second coming. In Chapter 5, I critiqued several pretribulation notions that purport a dichotomy between the rapture and the second coming. It was shown that these notions are an artificial, prejudicial construct. In Chapter 6, I demonstrated that the second coming does not begin with the battle of Armageddon. In this final chapter, I will contend that the second coming begins with the rapture, and as such, there is no intervening period between the rapture and the beginning of the second coming. To be sure, the rapture is not equated with the second coming. Instead, it is one of the very first events that will occur when the second coming starts. Deliverance and divine destruction will occur back to back when Jesus returns. This final chapter, then, will demonstrate the twofold point: (1) the second coming begins with the rapture, and (2) there is no intervening period between the rapture and the second coming.

First, I will establish that the second coming/ Parousia and the day of the Lord are co-referential. The New Testament writers used these two common descriptors to denote the same event interchangeably. Second, I will argue that the Parousia/day of the Lord starts with the rapture (and resurrection). I will begin with passages that relate the rapture to the usage of *parousia* (coming) and then turn to passages that relate the rapture to the usage of the expression *the day of the Lord*. I will conclude with the implication that key prophesied events will take place before the rapture. Consequently, the Parousia presupposition will be shown to be a flawed and an artificial foundation for pretribulationism.

The Co-reference between the Parousia and the Day of the Lord

When the Bible, especially in the New Testament, addresses Christ's return, two of the most common terms that denote this event are *parousia* (coming) and *hēmera kyriou* (day of the Lord). The New Testament writers understood these two descriptors as co-referential for Jesus's unified future second coming. They are not two separate events, but the same. Each term, however, possesses its own connotation depending on the context. The *day of the Lord* generally expresses the negative-judgment aspect of our Lord's return and the term parousia generally expresses the positive-redemptive aspect of our Lord's return. In this first section, I will address six biblical themes that illustrate how the New Testament authors interchangeably used the terms *parousia* and *hēmera kyriou*, the Greek terms behind coming and day of the Lord, respectively.

Destruction at the Parousia/day of the Lord:

> But the **day of the Lord** will come like a thief; when it comes, the heavens will disappear with a horrific noise, and the celestial bodies will melt away in a blaze, and the

> earth and every deed done on it will be laid bare. Since all these things are to melt away in this manner, what sort of people must we be, conducting our lives in holiness and godliness, while waiting for and hastening the **coming** of the day of God? Because of this day, the heavens will be burned up and dissolve, and the celestial bodies will melt away in a blaze! (2 Pet 3:10–12).

Exhortation to be blameless at the Parousia/day of the Lord:

> He will also strengthen you to the end, so that you will be blameless on the **day of our Lord Jesus Christ** (1 Cor 1:8).
> [S]o that you can decide what is best, and thus be sincere and blameless for the **day of Christ**[1] **[i.e. Lord]** (Phil 1:10).

1. Pretribulation interpreters maintain a difference in meaning between the *day of the Lord* and the *day of Christ*; e.g. Stanton, *Kept from the Hour*, 75; Scofield, *Reference Bible*, 1212. However, Pentecost (*Things to Come*, 232) is more inclined to view them co-referentially. The term *day of Christ* (Phil 1:6, 10, 2:16) has been thought to refer to the rapture and not God's wrath, while the *day of the Lord* is believed to refer to a different period concerned only with God's wrath. (Incidentally, the KJV in 2 Thess 2:2 has the reading "the day of Christ," but the earlier manuscripts overwhelmingly attest to the reading "the day of the Lord.") Both terms, however, should be understood to refer to the same event, being interchangeable designations for the unified extended-whole of Jesus's return. This does not mean that their respective contexts cannot constrain a certain aspect of Christ's return such as, for example, on the beginning point when the saints will meet Christ. Nor does it mean that they share the exact same connotation. No two words share the exact same connotation, but many words can *refer* to the same event, thing, or concept. The day of the Lord *includes* the day the rapture happens. Therefore, the distinction between the day of Christ and the day of the Lord is inconsequential to the rapture question. There are good reasons why both terms co-referentially denote the same event of our Lord's return. The Lord *is* Christ. The apostle Paul uses "Lord" for "Christ" innumerable times, and interpreting Old Testament prophecies concerning the day of the Lord to be *about Christ* is no exception. Thus, Paul had the freedom, especially as we see in Philippians, to interchange "Lord" for the church's new messianic understanding in "Christ" or "Jesus." A conflation of the two terms is found in 1 Cor 1:8: "He will also strengthen you to the end, so that you will be blameless on the *day of our Lord Jesus Christ*" (cf. 1 Cor 1:7!). A conflation is also found in 2 Cor 1:14: "day of the Lord Jesus." Using pretribulation

> So that your hearts are strengthened in holiness to be blameless before our God and Father at the **coming** of our Lord Jesus with all his saints (1 Thess 3:13, cf. 5:23).[2]

Resurrection will occur at the Parousia/Day of the Lord:

> For the Lord himself will come down from heaven with a shout of command, with the voice of the archangel, and with the trumpet of God, and the dead in Christ will rise first. . . . For you know quite well that the **day of the Lord** will come in the same way as a thief in the night (1 Thess 4:16—5:2). For I am sure of this very thing, that the one who began a good work in you will perfect it until the **day of Christ Jesus** (Phil 1:6, cf. 1 Cor 5:5, 2 Thess 1:10).
>
> But each in his own order: Christ, the firstfruits; then when Christ **comes**,[3] those who belong to him (1 Cor 15:23).

Boasting in labor will occur at the Parousia/Day of the Lord:

> [A]s you have understood us in part, you will come to understand fully that you can boast of us just as we will boast of you in the **day of the Lord Jesus** (2 Cor 1:14). [B]y holding on to the word of life so that on the **day of Christ** I will have a reason to boast that I did not run in vain nor labor in vain (Phil 2:16).
>
> For who is our hope or joy or crown to boast of before our Lord Jesus at his **coming**? Is it not of course you? (1 Thess 2:19).

---

logic, these four variations would denote four different periods! Robert H. Gundry (*Church and the Tribulation*, 98) makes the point that "if mere differences in titles and names justified distinctions, we ought to distinguish between 'the judgment-seat of God' (Rom. 14:10) and 'the judgment-seat of Christ' (2 Cor 5:10). Yet no one thinks of doing so." In my analysis below, I will give additional reasons why the rapture is included in the unified day of the Lord.

2. Cf. Nicholl, *From Hope to Despair in Thessalonica*, 51, n. 13; Kreitzer, *Jesus and God in Paul's Eschatology*, 112–29.

3. For readability, many English translations in this instance render the Greek noun *parousia* as a verb, "when Christ *comes*." The literal rendering, however, is "at his *coming*."

The Antichrist and apostasy will occur before the Parousia/ Day of the Lord:

> Now regarding the **coming**[4] of our Lord Jesus Christ and our being gathered to be with him, we ask you, brothers and sisters, not to be easily shaken from your composure or disturbed by any kind of spirit or message or letter allegedly from us, to the effect that the **day of the Lord** is already here. Let no one deceive you in any way. For that day will not arrive until the rebellion comes and the man of lawlessness is revealed, the son of destruction (2 Thess 2:1–3).

Back-to-back rapture and judgment at the Parousia/Day of the Lord:

> For we tell you this by the word of the Lord, that we who are alive, who are left until the **coming** of the Lord, will surely not go ahead of those who have fallen asleep. For the Lord himself will come down from heaven with a shout of command, with the voice of the archangel, and with the trumpet of God, and the dead in Christ will rise first. Then we who are alive, who are left, will be suddenly caught up together with them in the clouds to meet the Lord in the air. And so we will always be with the Lord. Therefore encourage one another with these words. Now on the topic of times and seasons, brothers and sisters, you have no need for anything to be written to you. For you know quite well that the **day of the Lord** will come in the same way as a thief in the night (1 Thess 4:15–5:2).[5]

In summary, this analysis illustrates that the terms *coming (parousia)* and the *day of the Lord (hēmera kyriou)*

---

4. Some translations render *parousia* as "arrival" to emphasize the beginning point of the Parousia.

5. It is unfortunate that this passage is disrupted by a chapter break. The discourse describes the single, unified return of Jesus as back-to-back deliverance and judgment. Placing a chapter break at 1 Thess 5:1 breaks up the unity and coherence on the topic of the return of Christ. Jesus's return will result in two consequents, but differing effects for believers and unbelievers.

are co-referential and describe different aspects of the single, unified return of Christ.[6]

Table 8
Co-referential Terms

Second Coming/ Parousia	Day of the Lord
Destruction	Destruction
Exhortation	Exhortation
Resurrection	Resurrection
Boasting	Boasting
The Antichrist and Apostasy	The Antichrist and Apostasy
Rapture and Judgment	Rapture and Judgment

The Second Coming Begins with the Rapture

In Part 2, I have been examining the relationship between the rapture and the second coming. In this chapter, I am expanding the analysis to include the question of whether there is an intervening period between these two events. This is an important question because if the rapture occurs on the same day as the second coming/day of the Lord, then it follows that a cluster of biblical prophecies will take place before the rapture; e.g. the celestial disturbances (Joel 2:30–31), Elijah's coming (Mal 4:5), the exclaming of "peace and safety" (1 Thess 5:2–3), and the apostasy and the revelation of the Antichrist (2 Thess 2:1–4). If this same-day principle is correct, it invalidates the pretribulational argument that,

6. Additionally, the term *parousia* is used with synonymous terms for the day of the Lord that describe eschatological judgment in James 5:8–9 ("*parousia*" / "the judge stands before the gates"), Matt 24:37, 39 ("parousia" / "just like the days of Noah"), and 2 Thess 2:8 ("*parousia*" / "the Lord will slay").

by definition, the second coming is signless. For instance, pretribulation exponent Thomas Ice claims: "An interval or gap of time is *needed* between the rapture and the second coming in order to facilitate many events predicted in the Bible in a timely manner" (emphasis mine).[7]

I will begin with Paul's Thessalonian instruction and then turn to Jesus's Olivet Discourse. Three passages from Paul link the resurrection and rapture to the Parousia. First, in Paul's magnificent resurrection passage in 1 Cor 15, he explains that one of the first divine purposes of the Parousia is the resurrection: "But each in his own order: Christ, the firstfruits; then when Christ comes [*parousia*], those who belong to him [will be resurrected]" (1 Cor 15:23). In this verse, there is an integral link between the resurrection and the Parousia of Christ. Paul does not disconnect the resurrection from the Parousia, let alone disconnect it by a seven-year intervening period. For Paul, there is no temporal, intervening period between the two. The resurrection, of course, is not the Parousia itself, but belongs to the unified extended event. The resurrection will be one of many divine purposes for Jesus's Parousia. Second, in 1 Thess 4:15–18, Paul connects the resurrection and rapture with the Parousia. Specifically, in 1 Thess 4:15, he writes, "For we tell you this by the word of the Lord, that we who are alive, who are left *until* the coming [*parousia*] of the Lord, will surely not go ahead of those who have fallen asleep" (cf. vv. 16–17). Paul clearly teaches that the last generation of the church—those who are alive in Christ—survive right up to the beginning of the Parousia: "who are left *until* the coming [*parousia*] of the Lord." Third, in his second letter to the Thessalonians, he again links the Parousia to the rapture: "Now regarding the coming [*parousia*] of our Lord Jesus Christ and our being gathered to be with him [the rapture], we ask you, brothers and sisters . . ."

7. Ice, "Why I Believe the Bible Teaches Rapture before Tribulation," http://www.pre-trib.org/articles/view/why-i-believe-bible-teaches-rapture-before-tribulation

(2 Thess 2:1). In all three passages, Paul links the resurrection and rapture with the Parousia.

In the previous chapter, I addressed the pretribulation claim that the *parousia* mentioned by Jesus in Matt 24 is a different *parousia* (or different phase of the Parousia) than the one that Paul taught in 1 Thess 4. I argued that there is no evidence that Paul addresses an "imminent rapture" coming, while Jesus addresses the "Armageddon coming" construed as the second coming. Pretribulationism cannot escape the point that both Paul and Jesus are speaking of the beginning of the one and only Parousia. Paul describes the initial aspect of the *parousia* by instructing that the resurrection and rapture will happen immediately when Christ comes back. The last generation of the church will survive up to the beginning of his coming. In Matt 24:27–31, Jesus also draws attention to the beginning of the *parousia* by instructing that the sign of this event (v. 27) will be his glory bursting through at his return (vv. 30–31). This sign will announce the *parousia*. He connects this with the gathering of the elect:

> "For just like the lightning comes from the east and flashes to the west, so the coming [*parousia*] of the Son of Man will be. Wherever the corpse is, there the vultures will gather. Immediately after the suffering of those days, the sun will be darkened, and the moon will not give its light; the stars will fall from heaven, and the powers of heaven will be shaken. Then the sign of the Son of Man will appear in heaven, and all the tribes of the earth will mourn. They will see the Son of Man arriving on the clouds of heaven with power and great glory. And he will send his angels with a loud trumpet blast, and they will *gather his elect from the four winds, from one end of heaven to the other*" (Matt 24:27–31).

Jesus's parables and similitudes corroborate this point through illustrating the beginning point of his Parousia (see Matt 24:37—25:30). It follows that the gathering of the elect is the rapture of the saints—the main reason that Paul draws from Jesus's discourse for his rapture teaching to the Thessalonians.[8] What immediately precedes the rapture is the great and glorious sign of the Son of Man in the sky that bursts through the darkening from the celestial disturbances. The sign signals to the world that the Son has returned. At that point, Jesus resurrects the dead in Christ and bestows new bodies to Christians alive at that time. Then both groups will be caught up together to meet Christ in the sky. Jesus and Paul consistently address the beginning point of the *parousia.*

There will not, therefore, be an intervening period between the rapture and the *parousia.* The deliverance of God's saints will be followed on the same day by God's judgment.[9] To maintain the pretribulation framework, an intervening period between the rapture and the Parousia is necessary. This supposed intervening period enables the pretribulation interpreter to place prophesied events only after the rapture. An intervening period is definitional for the Parousia presupposition.

The Day of the Lord Begins with the Rapture

In the first section, I explained that the Bible uses the terms *parousia* and *day of the Lord* co-referentially to denote the same period. In the second section, I described that the rapture is one of the first events of the Parousia. In this section, I will examine key passages that use the term the *day of the Lord* as it relates to the rapture for its first event.

As a preface, I need to describe a shift that is

---

8. For my full analysis as to why Matt 24:31 should be construed as the resurrection and the rapture, see Kurschner, *Antichrist Before the Day of the Lord*, 86–94.

9. In Rev 7:9–17, the innumerable multitude appears in heaven. This is followed by half an hour of silence before the unleashing of God's wrath: "Now when the Lamb opened the seventh seal there was silence in heaven for about half an hour" (Rev 8:1).

taking place within pretribulation theology. Traditional pretribulationism has consistently held that the rapture and the day of the Lord's wrath will occur back to back.[10] The day the rapture happens will be the same day that the day of the Lord's wrath *begins*. (Pretribulationalism locates the rapture before the start of the seven-year period, while prewrath does not.) A few traditional statements from pretribulation theologians will explain this point:

Henry A. Ironside: ". . . when at last the day of grace [the church age] is ended the day of the Lord will succeed it. . . . The day of the Lord follows [the rapture]."[11]

J. Dwight Pentecost: "The only way this day [of the Lord] could break unexpectedly upon the world is to have it begin immediately after the rapture of the church."[12]

John S. Feinberg: "According to pretribulationism, after the rapture the Tribulation begins."[13]

Robert L. Thomas: "The return of Christ for His church and the return of Christ to inflict wrath and tribulation on the world is close at hand and can happen at any moment."[14] [He also states,] "Only if the rapture coincides with the beginning of the day of the Lord can both be imminent and the salvation of those in Christ coincide with the

---

10. Some early pretribulationists, though viewing Daniel's seventieth week as God's wrath, construed the day of the Lord separately as the period from Armageddon to the end of the millennium (e.g. Scofield, *Reference Bible*, 1349; Gaebelein, *Harmony of the Prophetic Word*, 41). But most traditional pretribulation theologians, at least in the past century, have viewed the day of the Lord beginning with the rapture and spanning the entirety of Daniel's seventieth week.

11. Ironside, *James and Peter*, 98–99.

12. Pentecost, *Things to Come*, 230.

13. Feinberg, "Arguing about the Rapture," 200.

14. Thomas, "Rapture and the Biblical Teaching of Imminency," 24.

coming of wrath to the rest" (1 Thess 5:9).[15]

Kevin D. Zuber: "Since the rapture will take all living saints to be with the Lord at the same time that the day of the Lord commences, no believer need fear that he will be found in the day of the Lord."[16]

This traditional pretribulation tenet is consequential because prewrath eschatology points out that the following biblical prophecies will occur prior to the day of the Lord: the celestial disturbances (Joel 2:30–31), Elijah's coming (Mal 4:5), the exclaiming of "peace and safety" (1 Thess 5:2–3), and the apostasy and the revelation of the Antichrist (2 Thess 2:1–4).

Five Events Before the Day of the Lord

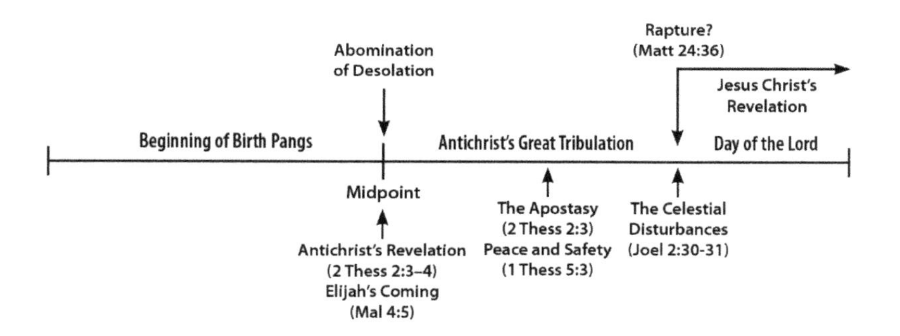

Since the rapture will occur the same day as the day of the Lord's wrath begins, it follows that these "day of the Lord" prophecies will occur before the rapture. Establishing this

15. Thomas, "1, 2 Thessalonians," 281.

16. Zuber, "Paul and the Rapture," 164; see also Blaising and Bock, *Progressive Dispensationalism*, 264; Darby, *Letters of J. N. D. Volume 3*, 424; Elmore, "J. N. Darby's Early Years," 137–38; Pentecost, *Things to Come*, 201; Ryrie, *Dispensationalism*, 148; Rydelnik, "Israel," 257; Patterson, "Israel and the Great Tribulation," 70.

point undermines the pretribulation notion of an "imminent" return of Jesus. A growing number of pretribulation interpreters are recognizing this valid prewrath objection. In response, they are reconfiguring their traditional pretribulation framework, depending on the particular pretribulation interpreter, by creating a gap of days, months, or years between the rapture and the day of the Lord either *within* the seven-year period or *before* the seven-year period. To maintain the imminence framework, the pretribulation interpreter must place these "before the day of the Lord" prophecies during this intervening gap. In either of these gap theories, the prophecies occur after the rapture but before the start of the day of the Lord.

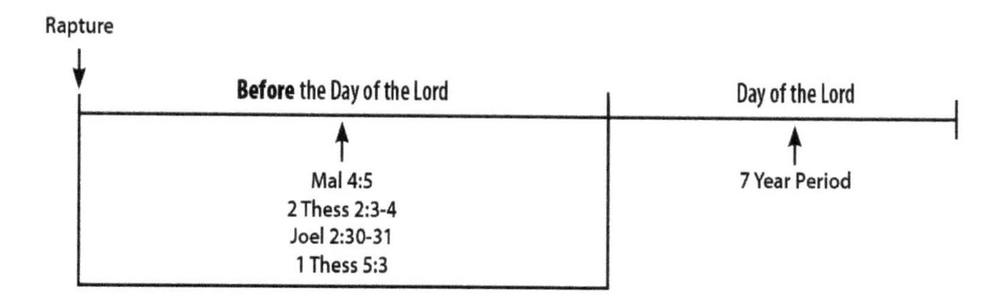

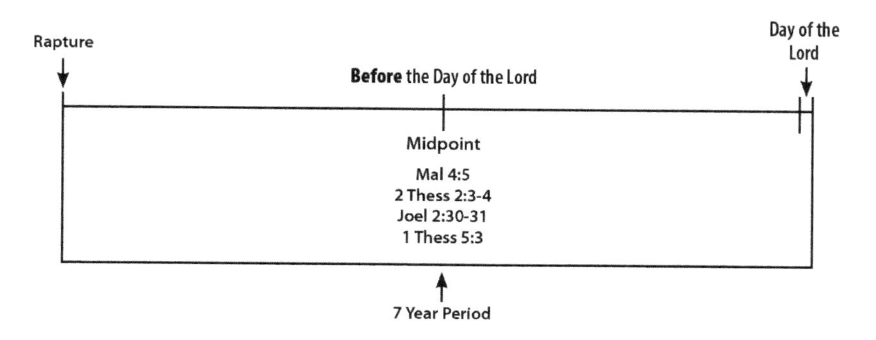

For example, pretribulation exponent Arnold G. Fruchtenbaum believes that the rapture will occur before a gap of time that will take place before Daniel's seventieth week begins. He reconfigures the traditional pretribulation framework by claiming that it is an "erroneous assumption that pretribulationism requires the rapture to occur just before, or at the start of, the seven years."[17]

The pretribulation "gap proposal" is deeply flawed, forced, and contradicts the biblical evidence. In the following, I will set out to explain that the same day the rapture happens, the day the Lord's judgments begin. Key passages are examined that use "day of the Lord" language to describe Christ returning to rapture his people on the very day that God's judgments begin. Those judgments, of course, are not limited to a single day but unfold over an undetermined length of time (e.g. the fifth trumpet occurs for five months). The following analysis of these "day of the Lord" passages will provide additional corroboration to the "back-to-back" process.

The Day of the Lord According to Paul

There is a biblical pattern in which God supernaturally rescues his people immediately before he executes divine judgment. This is memorably portrayed in the story of the Egyptian plagues, culminating in the deliverance of Israel from the hands of Pharaoh's army that was ultimately destroyed in the Red Sea. This pattern continues in the context of the eschatological day of the Lord. Paul gives believers the reassuring promise: "For God did not destine us for wrath but for gaining salvation through our Lord Jesus Christ" (1 Thess 5:9). The term for "salvation" in this verse is

17. Fruchtenbaum, "Is There a Pre-Wrath Rapture?" 395. Fruchtenbaum claims that he has always held to a gap view (395). Regardless, pretribulationists are exchanging their traditional view for a gap framework (see also Salus, *Next Prophecies*, 33–37); cf. Olander, "Pre-Day of the Lord Rapture," 272–73.

sōtēria. It can have two common meanings: salvation in the sense of physical deliverance and salvation in the sense of non-physical deliverance, such as spiritual salvation. Here it takes on the former meaning since this promise relates to the rapture and the day of the Lord; thus, for believers, the day of the Lord will not "overtake you like a thief" (1 Thess 5:4).

The day of the Lord is not a twenty-four-hour day but rather a unified, extended event, encompassing the deliverance of the saints, divine judgments, Israel's salvation, and the establishment of Jesus's earthly kingdom. In 1 Thess 5:1–11, Paul teaches that the last generation of the church will exist up to the first day of the day of the Lord. On the first day, the Lord will deliver the church via the rapture from the ensuing day of the Lord's wrath. In his first epistle to the Thessalonians, the apostle Paul furnished us with one of the most important biblical teachings on the day of the Lord.

> Now on the topic of times and seasons, brothers and sisters, you have no need for anything to be written to you. For you know quite well that the day of the Lord will come in the same way as a thief in the night. Now when they are saying, "There is peace and security," then sudden destruction comes on them, like labor pains on a pregnant woman, and they will surely not escape. But you, brothers and sisters, are not in the darkness for the day to overtake you like a thief would. For you all are sons of the light and sons of the day. We are not of the night nor of the darkness. So then we must not sleep as the rest, but must stay alert and sober. For those who sleep, sleep at night and those who get drunk are drunk at night. But since we are of the day, we must stay sober by putting on the breastplate of faith and love and as a helmet our hope for salvation. For God did not destine us for wrath but for gaining salvation through our Lord Jesus Christ. He died for us so that whether we are alert or asleep we will come to life together with him. Therefore encourage one another and build up each other, just as you are in fact doing (1 Thess 5:1–11).

In the immediate context of 1 Thess 4:13–18, Paul responded to the hopeless grieving of the Thessalonians by correcting an important point in their eschatology as it relates to the rapture and resurrection. Evidently, that was not the only element of defective eschatology that Paul had to correct for this young church. The Thessalonians were feeling trepidation that they might experience divine judgment. Accordingly, in 1 Thess 5:1–11, Paul reassures them of God's promise and sovereignty in their election, while explaining how the return of Jesus will affect unbelievers. The chapter break at 5:1 is unfortunate since ch. 4 is part of the same unified, coherent message. 1 Thessalonians 4–5 is a cohesive text that relates the hope of Christ's return to God's judgment of the unrighteous. Colin R. Nicholl provides six reasons for the cohesion between 1 Thess 4:13–18 and 1 Thess 5:1–11:[18]

1. Both relate to the fate of believers at the eschaton and both reflect an "apocalyptic" conceptual framework.

2. They have a similar structure: the topic statement with *adelphoi* (4:13; 5:1), the essential reply (4:14; 5:2), and the paraenetic [moral instruction] conclusion (4:18; 5:11).

3. 5:10's *eite katheudōmen* ["or asleep"] recalls 4:13–18, while *eite grēgorōmen* ["or alive"] seems to allude to the problem underlying 5:11ff.

4. Jesus's death and resurrection are the basis for confidence regarding eschatological destiny in both (4:14a; 5:9–10).

5. "Being with Christ" is the eschatological goal in both (4:17b; 5:10).

6. Both have the same function of reassuring/encouraging the community members (4:18; 5:11), and indeed 5:11 may well function to conclude 4:13ff.

---

18. Nicholl, *Hope to Despair*, 73.

Another reason Paul is not establishing a completely new topic at the chapter break in 1 Thess 5:1 is given by Douglas J. Moo:

> [O]bserve how Paul speaks of "times and dates" in verse 1 without specifying the time or date of *what*. The omission of any specific event here could indicate that the previous topic is in mind (emphasis his).[19]

The disruption of the unified discourse with the chapter break could mislead the interpreter to think that Paul is teaching two different types of comings of Jesus with a temporal gap between them. We should, therefore, keep in mind that chapter breaks are often misleading, lest we think Paul is starting a new topic at ch. 5.

In addition, Paul introduces 1 Thess 5:1–11 with the Greek phrase *peri de* ("now on the topic"). This phrase indicates that Paul is responding to a question already raised by the Thessalonians, revealing further confusion resulting from their defective eschatology. In other words, the phrase *peri de* does not mean that Paul is introducing a topic unrelated to his previous discussion on the Parousia. It does not have the technical meaning of "what comes before it, is disconnected from what comes after it." It simply means that Paul is beginning to shift to another perspective or topic that may be related to what came before. Only context can inform the interpreter of the nature of the shift, not the phrase itself. In this context, Paul is not addressing two completely different topics. Instead, he develops his discussion of the return of the Lord, showing its effects upon the godly *and* the ungodly. In ch. 4, Paul comforts the Thessalonian believers about the destiny of their dead loved ones and how the return of Jesus will affect believers. In ch. 5, he turns to explain how Jesus's return will affect unbelievers, while exhorting believers about their own position in Christ in light of his return. Paul instructs

19. Moo, *Three Views on the Rapture*, 202.

that Jesus's return will involve back-to-back deliverance and judgment. With reference to unbelievers, he explains that they will not be able to escape the sudden return of the Lord because they are spiritually unprepared and, consequently, will experience God's eschatological wrath.

Paul's then makes the point in 1 Thess 5:4 that believers who are living at that time will not be caught off guard: "But you, brothers and sisters, are not in the darkness for the day to overtake you like a thief would." Believers are instructed to watch for the day of the Lord because it will be salvation for saints living at that time, but judgment for the world:

> So then we must not sleep as the rest, but must stay alert [*grēgoreō*] and sober. For those who sleep, sleep at night and those who get drunk are drunk at night. But since we are of the day, we must stay sober by putting on the breastplate of faith and love and as a helmet our hope for salvation. For God did not destine us for wrath but for gaining salvation through our Lord Jesus Christ (1 Thess 5:6–9).

It would not make sense for Paul to instruct the Thessalonians to "stay alert" for the day of the Lord if the saints will be raptured before a gap. Paul reassures the Thessalonians that when the day of the Lord begins, all saints "whether we are alert [alive and watching] or asleep [dead in Christ] we will come to life [resurrection] together with him [raptured]" (1 Thess 5:10, cf. 1 Thess 4:14–18). The last generation of the church, therefore, will be here for the beginning of the day of the Lord when Christ delivers the saints the day that the earthly judgments begin. In short, the day of the Lord denotes the Lord's unified return, which includes the rapture and the execution of God's wrath upon the wicked.

In Paul's second letter to the Thessalonians, he reinforces this same-day occurrence with two statements. First, in 2 Thess 1:6–10, Paul describes the hope that God's people will be given relief from their tribulations. This will occur on the same day that God's judgment begins for unbelievers:

> For it is right for God to repay with affliction those who afflict you, and to you who are being afflicted to give rest together with us when the Lord Jesus is revealed from heaven with his mighty angels. With flaming fire he will mete out punishment on those who do not know God and do not obey the gospel of our Lord Jesus. They will undergo the penalty of eternal destruction, away from the presence of the Lord and from the glory of his strength, when he comes to be glorified among his saints and admired *on that day* among all who have believed—and you did in fact believe our testimony.

In 2 Thess 1:7, Paul prophecies that the church will experience affliction right up to when the revelation of Christ begins: "and to you who are being afflicted to give rest together with us when the Lord Jesus is revealed from heaven with his mighty angels." Then he explains that two things will happen on the day the revelation of Christ begins. First, believers will be given "rest" (i.e. delivered). This is certainly a reference to Paul's previous rapture teaching in 1 Thess 4:13–18 when God's people will experience deliverance at Jesus's return. Second, the day they are given rest will be "when the Lord Jesus is revealed from heaven with his mighty angels. With flaming fire he will mete out punishment on those who do not know God and do not obey the gospel of our Lord Jesus" (2 Thess 1:7–8). Paul is making a reference back to his first epistle with regard to the day of the Lord's wrath that will immediately follow the rapture (1 Thess 5:1–9). Paul reiterates this point, explaining that he will begin to judge the ungodly "on that day" when the godly are united with Christ: "They will undergo the penalty of eternal destruction, away from the presence of the Lord and from the glory of his strength, when he comes to be glorified among his saints and admired on that day among all who have believed—and you did in fact believe our testimony" (2 Thess 1:9–10). For believers alive at that time "who believe our testimony" (v. 10), that day will begin eternal rest; while for unbelievers who "do not obey the gospel" (v. 8), it will begin eternal unrest. There will not be a delay of days or longer between the rapture of the righteous and the onset to the day of the Lord's judgment upon the ungodly. The Lord's coming will be twofold: back-to-back deliverance and judgment.

The second same-day statement in Paul's second letter to the Thessalonians is found at 2 Thess 2:1–2, where he restates this connection by again linking the gathering of the saints with the day of the Lord: "Now regarding the coming of our Lord Jesus Christ and our *being gathered to be with him* [the rapture], we ask you, brothers and sisters, not to be easily shaken from your composure or disturbed by any kind of spirit or message or letter allegedly from us, to the effect that the day of the Lord is already here." Paul again relates the gathering of the saints (rapture) to the coming of the day of the Lord. When Jesus returns to deliver God's saints, he will mete out wrath upon the wicked.

Pretribulationist Richard Mayhue, however, thinks that Paul does not teach a back-to-back occurrence of the rapture and wrath. He writes,

> Paul is not writing a detailed, chronological, or even precise prophetic treatise here, but rather is wanting to give the Thessalonians hope that, in the end, God's righteousness would prevail. Like Old Testament prophets (cf. Isa 61:1–2, 2 Pet 1:10–11), Paul has compressed the details so that the range of time is not apparent, nor are all of the details. The apostle is plainly assuring the Thessalonians that there will certainly be a coming day of retribution for their persecutors. As a result, this text has no bearing on determining the time of the rapture.[20]

---

20. Mayhue, "Why a Pretribulation Rapture?," 101.

We can agree with Mayhue on two points. First, it is correct that Paul did not intend to write a detailed account of God's wrath, as if it all occurs within a twenty-four-hour day. Paul is compressing the details for the purpose of giving a summary statement on judgment. He is highlighting the point that when Christ returns there will be two immediate consequences: the saints being delivered and the wicked being judged. Paul is emphasizing judgment *qua* judgment and not intending to describe the full account of the extended series of judgment elements. Second, we can agree with Mayhue that Paul is giving "hope that, in the end, God's righteousness would prevail" and "assuring the Thessalonians that there will certainly be a coming day of retribution for their persecutors." We must, however, disagree with Mayhue's assertion that Paul does not use temporal language. Paul uses explicit temporal language by chronologically tying together deliverance and judgment: "when" and "on that day." In fact, the "hope" that Paul is seeking to foster for the trepidatious Thessalonians is grounded in the promise that God will begin to judge their persecutors on the same day as the deliverance of the godly. Paul could not describe it more plainly: When Jesus is revealed from heaven "to give rest" to his afflicted saints, he will be accompanied "with his mighty angels" with "flaming fire to mete out punishment" upon the wicked. Mayhue's interpretation of Paul, then, is flawed and ignores this key point in Paul's instruction.

The Day of the Lord According to Jesus

Having examined Paul's teaching on this topic, Jesus's portrayal is, not surprisingly, consistent on this point, that eschatological deliverance and judgment will occur back to back. In the Olivet Discourse, Jesus instructs that there will be an immediate eschatological separation at his return:

> "Then the sign of the Son of Man will appear in heaven, and

> all the tribes of the earth will mourn. They will see the Son of Man arriving on the clouds of heaven with power and great glory. And he will send his angels with a loud trumpet blast, and they will gather his elect from the four winds, from one end of heaven to the other" (Matt 24:30–31).

In Matt 24:37—25:30, Jesus illustrates this separation event between the elect and the non-elect with a cluster of vivid similitudes and parables that reinforce the same-day principle (e.g. Noahic flood, one taken and the other left, owner of the house, ten virgins). Luke's parallel account also portrays the back-to-back nature of the deliverance of God's people and judgment upon the world:

> "And there will be signs in the sun and moon and stars, and on the earth nations will be in distress, anxious over the roaring of the sea and the surging waves. People will be fainting from fear and from the expectation of what is coming on the world, for the powers of the heavens will be shaken. Then they will see the Son of Man arriving in a cloud with power and great glory. But when these things begin to happen, stand up and raise your heads, because your redemption is drawing near" (Luke 21:25–28).

> "But be on your guard so that your hearts are not weighed down with dissipation and drunkenness and the worries of this life, and that day close down upon you suddenly like a trap. For it will overtake all who live on the face of the whole earth. But stay alert at all times, praying that you may have strength to escape all these things that must happen, and to stand before the Son of Man" (Luke 21:34–36).

An explicit account of the back-to-back, same-day occurrence is also described in another of Luke's eschatological accounts where Jesus draws from the Noahic narrative:

> "The days are coming when you will desire to see one of the days of the Son of Man, and you will not see it. Then people will say to you, 'Look, there he is!' or 'Look, here he is!' Do not go out or chase after them. For just like the lightning

> flashes and lights up the sky from one side to the other, so will the Son of Man be in his day. But first he must suffer many things and be rejected by this generation. Just as it was in the days of Noah, so too it will be in the days of the Son of Man. People were eating, they were drinking, they were marrying, they were being given in marriage—*right up to the day Noah entered the ark. Then the flood came and destroyed them all*" (Luke 17:22–27 emphasis mine, cf. Matt 24:37–41).

In this passage, there are at least three important truths regarding Christ's return. First, the sign of his second coming will be like lightning that lights up the sky (cf. Matt 24:3, 27, 30). This will be his glory announcing his divine presence to the entire world. Second, Jesus likens unbelievers at the time of his second coming to those at the time of the flood. In referring to the time of the flood, Jesus says people were going on with their everyday affairs of eating, drinking, marrying, and being given in marriage. He does not refer to gluttony, drunkenness, and immorality. To be sure, the antediluvian world was egregiously God-hating and self-loving (Gen 6:11–13), and it is safe to assume that they were engaging in gluttony, drunkenness, and immorality (2 Pet 2:5). But in this passage, that is not the point Jesus is making, even though there would have been connotations evoked from his audience. He is highlighting that they were going on with their everyday, normal activities, indifferent to and oblivious to God's impending wrath. In short, the people in Noah's day were unprepared when the flood came. So will it be in the days when Christ comes. People will be going on with their everyday business, living only to please themselves. Similarly, Paul teaches that at the onset of the day of the Lord, unbelievers will have been saying, "peace and security" as "sudden destruction comes on them, like labor pains on a pregnant woman, and they will surely not escape" (1 Thess 5:3). The third point Jesus makes, and the one mostly relevant to our discussion, is that the obliviousness from Noah's generation occurred "right up to the day" Noah entered the ark. The same day they entered, the flood began, not two days nor five days nor seven days later—the very same day. The deluge began the very day Noah and his family entered the ark and shut the door (Gen 7:1–18). Noah was told that he had seven days to corral the animals because the Lord warned, "in seven days I will cause it to rain" (Gen 7:4). At the end of the seven days, "all the fountains of the great deep burst open and the floodgates of the heavens were opened" (Gen 7:11). This happened "on that very day Noah entered the ark" (Gen 7:13).

Drawing from Jesus's Noahic analogy, we can conclude that there will not be a gap of days, weeks, months, or years between the deliverance of the saints and the unleashing of God's wrath. It will be back to back, beginning on the same day. One of the main purposes of delivering God's saints is to protect them from his judgment. To make sure he is not misunderstood about this truth, Jesus reinforces this point with the story of Lot and Sodom:

> "Likewise, just as it was in the days of Lot, people were eating, drinking, buying, selling, planting, building; but *on the day* Lot went out from Sodom, fire and sulfur rained down from heaven and destroyed them all. *It will be the same on the day* the Son of Man is revealed. *On that day*, anyone who is on the roof, with his goods in the house, must not come down to take them away, and likewise the person in the field must not turn back. Remember Lot's wife! Whoever tries to keep his life will lose it, but whoever loses his life will preserve it. I tell you, in that night there will be two people in one bed; one will be taken and the other left. There will be two women grinding grain together; one will be taken and the other left" (Luke 17:28–35).

In the days of Lot—just as in the days of Noah—people were going on with their everyday tasks, "eating, drinking, buying, selling, planting, building." They were unaware of and unprepared for God's impending judgment. His judgment began on the same day of Lot's deliverance: "On the day Lot went out from Sodom, fire and sulfur rained down from heaven and destroyed them all" (cf. Gen 19:23–28). Accordingly, "it will be the same on the day the Son of Man is revealed."

Some pretribulation teachers recognize the weight of this argument but continue to maintain an intervening period between the rapture and the day of the Lord's wrath.[21] A common objection claims that the flood narrative depicts Noah entering the ark, not on the same day the flood begins, but seven days before it. It has been argued that the seven days are a type of the future seventieth week of Daniel, with the rapture corresponding to the deliverance of Noah's family before the flood begins. But this typology is assumed, not proven. For example, Arnold G. Fruchtenbaum asserts,

> [T]he statement is *not* true in reference to Noah. Luke 17:27 simply states "that Noah entered into the ark, and the flood came, and destroyed them all." There is nothing Jesus said that implies that the judgment came "on the same day" that Noah entered the ark [emphasis his].[22]

He is demonstrably mistaken. The day Noah enters the ark, God initiated his judgment. Fruchtenbaum misquotes Luke 17:27, which explicitly reads, "People were eating, they were drinking, they were marrying, they were being given in marriage—*right up to the day* Noah entered the ark. Then the flood came and destroyed them all." Fruchtenbaum leaves out the key point: "right up to the day." He is ignoring Jesus's plain words when he claims, "There is nothing Jesus said that implies that the judgment came 'on the same day' that Noah

21. E.g. Karleen, *Pre-Wrath Rapture*, 66–67; Mayhue, "The Bible's Watchword," 83–88; McLean "Another Look," 394.

22. Fruchtenbaum, "Is There a Pre-Wrath Rapture?" 392.

entered the ark." In addition, Jesus makes the same point with the Lot episode and concludes: "It will be the same *on the day* the Son of Man is revealed" (Luke 17:30).

Next, Fruchtenbaum writes,

> In fact, Genesis 7:10 states that the waters of the flood began seven days *after* Noah entered the ark, and then continued forty days. The flood did not come the same day that Noah entered the ark, nor was all flesh destroyed in that day. [. . .] Just as there was a period of time between Noah entering the ark and the start of the rain, so there can also be a period of time between the rapture and the start of the seven years (emphasis his).[23]

He is mistaken again. The text does not say that the flood began seven days after Noah entered the ark, as if there were a seven-day delay from the time Noah's family entered the ark and when the flood rains began. Genesis 7:10 reads, "[A]fter seven days the floodwaters engulfed the earth." Fruchtenbaum is assuming that the seven days began after Noah and his family entered the ark. But the context states that the seven days refers to God's command to Noah to gather animals into the ark *before seven days came to pass.* Here is the context of v. 10:

> The LORD said to Noah, "Come into the ark, you and all your household, for I consider you godly among this generation. You must take with you seven of every kind of clean animal, the male and its mate, two of every kind of unclean animal, the male and its mate, and also seven of every kind of bird in the sky, male and female, to preserve their offspring on the face of the earth. *For in seven days I will cause it to rain* on the earth for forty days and forty nights, and I will wipe from the face of the ground every living thing that I have made." And Noah did all that the LORD commanded him. Noah was 600 years old when the

---

23. Fruchtenbaum, "Is There a Pre-Wrath Rapture?" 392–93.

> floodwaters engulfed the earth. Noah entered the ark along with his sons, his wife, and his sons' wives because of the floodwaters. Pairs of clean animals, of unclean animals, of birds, and of everything that creeps along the ground, male and female, came into the ark to Noah, just as God had commanded him. *And after seven days* the floodwaters engulfed the earth (Gen 7:1–10).

The narrative reveals, therefore, that "seven days" refers to the period for Noah to corral the animals into the ark before the seven days are completed. It does not depict Noah's family entering the ark seven days before the flood began. That is the time frame for Noah to corral the animals. Fruchtenbaum is massively reading his preconceived idea into the narrative, which alters the biblical story.

Moreover, if one continues to read further into the narrative context, it becomes explicitly clear that the exact day Noah and his family entered the ark was the day the flood-judgment began:

> In the six hundredth year of Noah's life, in the second month, on the seventeenth day of the month—*on that day all the fountains of the great deep burst open and the floodgates of the heavens were opened.* And the rain fell on the earth forty days and forty nights. *On that very day Noah entered the ark*, accompanied by his sons Shem, Ham, and Japheth, along with his wife and his sons' three wives (Gen 7:11–13).

The very day "the fountains of the great deep burst open and the floodgates of the heavens were opened" was the "very day Noah entered the ark." Jesus referenced back to the Genesis account when he said, "right up to the day Noah entered the ark. Then the flood came and destroyed them all." Jesus's application of the flood story likening to his own future coming is faithful to the Genesis account and fitting for his purpose. Deliverance of his people and the onset of judgment will occur back to back—on the very same day.

Rapture and God's Wrath – Back to Back

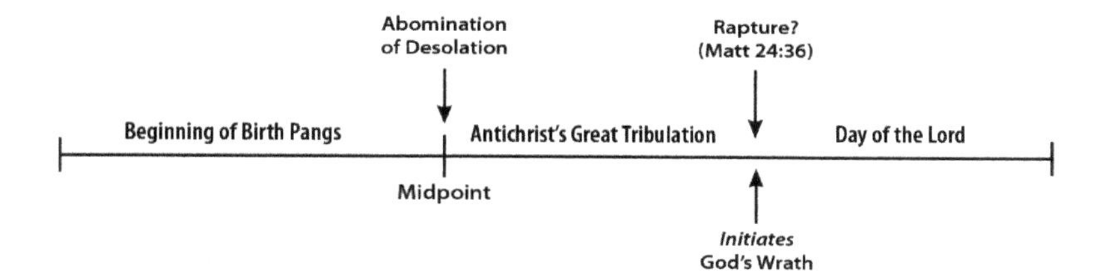

Conclusion

In this last chapter, I first established that the second coming (Parousia) and the day of the Lord are co-referential; the New Testament writers used these two designators interchangeably. I also argued that the rapture will be God's first divine purpose for the second coming/day of the Lord. Finally, I demonstrated that there is no intervening period of days, weeks, months, or years between the rapture and the start of God's eschatological wrath. They will be back-to-back events. The major implication of this chapter demonstrates that key prophesied events will happen before the rapture. These key events include:

> **A cluster of celestial signs:** I will produce portents both in the sky and on the earth—blood, fire, and columns of smoke. The sunlight will be turned to darkness and the moon to the color of blood, *before* the day of the LORD comes—that great and terrible day! (Joel 2:30–31).
>
> **The coming of Elijah:** Look, I will send you Elijah the prophet *before* the great and terrible day of the LORD arrives (Mal 4:5).
>
> **Claims of peace and security:** For you know quite well that the day of the Lord will come in the same way as a thief in the night. Now when they are saying, "There is peace and security," *then* [*tote*] sudden destruction comes on them, like labor pains on a pregnant woman, and they will surely

not escape (1 Thess 5:2–3).

The revealing of the Antichrist: Now regarding the arrival of our Lord Jesus Christ and our being gathered to be with him, we ask you, brothers and sisters, not to be easily shaken from your composure or disturbed by any kind of spirit or message or letter allegedly from us, to the effect that the day of the Lord is already here. Let no one deceive you in any way. For that day will not arrive until ["first," *proton*] the rebellion comes and the man of lawlessness is revealed, the son of destruction. He opposes and exalts himself above every so-called god or object of worship, and as a result he takes his seat in God's temple, displaying himself as God (2 Thess 2:1–4, cf. Matt 24:15–31).

In summary of Part 2, I followed several lines of reasoning. Chapter 4 described key terms that the New Testament authors used to picture the unified-whole of the extended series of events with the second coming. Chapter 5 critiqued several pretribulation notions that disconnect the rapture from the second coming. It was shown that these notions or "contrasts" are artificial constructs. Chapter 6 demonstrated that the second coming does not begin with the battle of Armageddon. Chapter 7 rounded out the evidence establishing that the second coming/day of the Lord begins with the rapture, with no intervening period. Deliverance and divine destruction will occur back to back. The evidence in Part 2 renders the Parousia presupposition a fractured foundation. The second coming begins with the event of the rapture.

Conclusion

In the introduction of this book, I outlined the two foundations of pretribulation theology, followed by a sketch of its history, then explained why this critique matters in the first place. In Part 1, I examined the ecclesiastical presupposition, the first of two foundational presuppositions in pretribulation theology. Chapter 1 described the presupposition within the larger theology of traditional dispensationalism, sketching its history and distinctives. Chapter 2 focused on the pretribulation interpretation of Daniel's prophecy from Dan 9:24–27, which is the traditional dispensational proof text for pretribulationism. Chapter 3 addressed the major tenet of the ecclesiastical presupposition in which God does not work with Israel and the church at the same time.

In Part 2, I turned to examine the second major pretribulation foundation, the Parousia presupposition. This foundational belief disconnects the rapture from the second coming. While the ecclesiastical presupposition creates the foundational hermeneutic principle for traditional pretribulationism concerning the temporal activities of Israel and the church, the Parousia presupposition creates the hermeneutic principle concerning the relation between the rapture and the second coming/Parousia. Part 2 argued that the rapture *belongs* to the second coming; it will occur at the beginning of this glorious event. Chapter 4 described key terms that the New Testament authors used to describe the unified extended-whole of the second coming. Chapter 5 critiqued several pretribulation notions that disconnect the rapture from the second coming. Chapter 6 argued that the second coming does not begin with the battle of Armageddon, but at an earlier point. Finally, Chapter 7 rounded out Part 2 by arguing that the second coming begins with the key event of the rapture, militating against the notion of a gap between the rapture and the second coming/day of the Lord. The rapture is not disconnected from the second coming; nor is it equated with it. Instead, the rapture is one of the very first events that will occur within the unified extended event of the second coming. In this study, I have explained there are two consequences resulting from the examination of these foundations. First, pretribulation rapture theology lacks a biblical foundation. Second, the implication is that the prophecies of the precursors that take place before the day of the Lord will in fact occur before the rapture (Joel 2:30–31; Mal 4:5; 1 Thess 5:2–3; 2 Thess 2:1–4).

Appendix 1

A BRIEF EXPLANATION OF THE PREWRATH VIEW

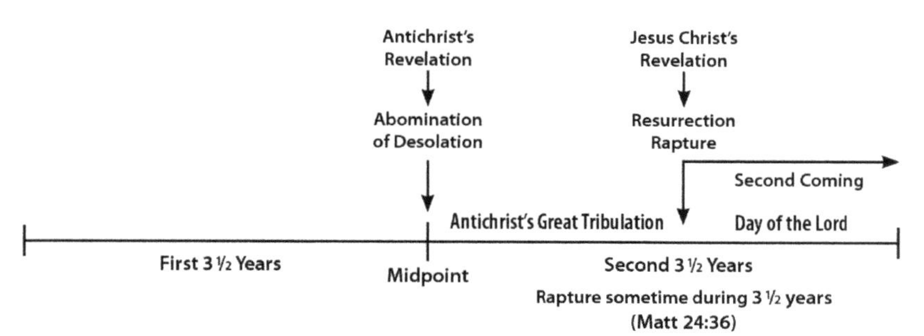

The following outline is intended only to adumbrate the prewrath viewpoint. I encourage the reader to become conversant with the position through a book-length treatment; for example, see my *Antichrist Before the Day of the Lord: What Every Christian Needs to Know about the Return of Christ* (Pompton Lakes, NJ: Eschatos Publishing, 2013). See also the slimdown version *Prewrath: A Very Short Introduction to the Great Tribulation, Rapture, and Day of the Lord* (Pompton Lakes, NJ: Eschatos Publishing, 2014).

Many of us have been told that the church will be "raptured out of here before the Antichrist's arrival." The

Bible, instead, teaches that the church will first experience the Antichrist's great tribulation. At some unknown hour or day, the great tribulation will be cut short by the return of Christ to resurrect and rapture believers before the day of the Lord's wrath—hence, prewrath. The church will suffer greatly just before Christ's second coming; the purging and purifying that will occur during this time will separate out those who claim to have faith from those who possess true faith.

Nowhere are Christians promised protection from tribulation. Rather, we are promised deliverance from God's wrath. Prewrath distinguishes the events of the Antichrist's great tribulation from the day of the Lord's wrath. The Antichrist's great tribulation will be directed against the church, which will be followed by the day of the Lord's wrath directed against the ungodly. The apostle Paul encapsulates this point in his second letter to the Thessalonians:

> Now regarding the arrival of our Lord Jesus Christ and our being gathered to be with him, we ask you, brothers and sisters, not to be easily shaken from your composure or disturbed by any kind of spirit or message or letter allegedly from us, to the effect that the day of the Lord is already here. Let no one deceive you in any way. For that day will not arrive until the rebellion comes and the man of lawlessness [the Antichrist] is revealed, the son of destruction (2 Thess 2:1–3).

The Antichrist's Great Tribulation

The "abomination of desolation" precipitates the great tribulation (Matt 24:15, 21). Jesus, drawing from the prophet Daniel, uses the expression "abomination of desolation" to personify the Antichrist figure as a detestable idol that causes sacrilege (Dan 9:27, 12:11). Paul gives further description to the activities of the Antichrist ("the man of lawlessness") at the midpoint of the seventieth week:

> He opposes and exalts himself above every so-called god or object of worship, and as a result he takes his seat in God's temple, displaying himself as God (2 Thess 2:4, cf. Dan 7:25, 11:36, Rev 13:5–6).

Jesus, Paul, and the book of Revelation warn of the satanic deception of signs and wonders associated with the Antichrist (Matt 24:24, 2 Thess 2:9, Rev 13:13–14). The Antichrist's great tribulation against believers, Jesus says, will be "unlike anything that has happened from the beginning of the world until now, or ever will happen" (Matt 24:21, cf. Rev 13). Believers will be persecuted because they will refuse to follow the Antichrist:

> If anyone is meant for captivity, into captivity he will go. If anyone is to be killed by the sword, then by the sword he must be killed. This requires steadfast endurance and faith from the saints (Rev 13:10, cf. Rev 14:9–13).

So great the martyrdom that Jesus says, "And if those days had not been cut short, no one would be saved. But for the sake of the elect those days will be cut short" (Matt 24:22, cf. 2 Thess 1:7). It is no wonder that the fifth seal martyrs cry out to God, "How long, Sovereign Master, holy and true, before you judge those who live on the earth and avenge our blood?" (Rev 6:10).

The Celestial Disturbances

God hears their prayers and cuts short the great tribulation by the return of his Son to deliver his people and execute his wrath upon the wicked. Just before this occurs, Jesus says a cluster of celestial events will take place:

> "Immediately after the tribulation of those days the sun will be darkened, and the moon will not give its light, and the stars will fall from heaven, and the powers of the heavens will be shaken" (Matt 24:29 ESV).

Jesus draws from the prophet Joel, who explicitly

prophesies that these celestial disturbances will happen before the day of the Lord comes:

> I will produce portents both in the sky and on the earth—blood, fire, and columns of smoke. The sunlight will be turned to darkness and the moon to the color of blood, *before* the day of the LORD comes—that great and terrible day! (Joel 2:30–31).

For the ungodly, the celestial disturbances signal impending wrath:

> "And there will be signs in the sun and moon and stars, and on the earth nations will be in distress, anxious over the roaring of the sea and the surging waves. People will be fainting from fear and from the expectation of what is coming on the world, for the powers of the heavens will be shaken" (Luke 21:25–26).

> Then I looked when the Lamb opened the sixth seal, and a huge earthquake took place; the sun became as black as sackcloth made of hair, and the full moon became blood red; and the stars in the sky fell to the earth like a fig tree dropping its unripe figs when shaken by a fierce wind. The sky was split apart like a scroll being rolled up, and every mountain and island was moved from its place. Then the kings of the earth, the very important people, the generals, the rich, the powerful, and everyone, slave and free, hid themselves in the caves and among the rocks of the mountains. They said to the mountains and to the rocks, "Fall on us and hide us from the face of the one who is seated on the throne and from the wrath of the Lamb, because the great day of their wrath has come, and who is able to withstand it?" (Rev 6:12–17).

The Resurrection and Rapture

For the saints, however, the celestial disturbances signal impending deliverance:

> "Then they will see the Son of Man arriving in a cloud with power and great glory. But when these things begin to happen, stand up and raise your heads, because your redemption is drawing near" (Luke 21:27–28).

When Christ appears in the sky in all his splendid glory, his angels will deliver the saints from the great tribulation by gathering them into the sky:

> "And he will send his angels with a loud trumpet blast, and they will gather his elect from the four winds, from one end of heaven to the other" (Matt 24:31).

The apostle Paul expands on this gathering using explicit resurrection and rapture language:

> For we tell you this by the word of the Lord, that we who are alive, who are left until the coming of the Lord, will surely not go ahead of those who have fallen asleep. For the Lord himself will come down from heaven with a shout of command, with the voice of the archangel, and with the trumpet of God, and the dead in Christ will rise first. Then we who are alive, who are left, will be suddenly caught up together with them in the clouds to meet the Lord in the air. And so we will always be with the Lord (1 Thess 4:15–17).

In the book of Revelation, we see the *effect* of the rapture: the sudden appearance in heaven of a great multitude described as coming "out of the great tribulation":

> After these things I looked, and here was an enormous crowd that no one could count, made up of persons from every nation, tribe, people, and language, standing before the throne and before the Lamb dressed in long white robes, and with palm branches in their hands. They were shouting out in a loud voice, "Salvation belongs to our God, to the one seated on the throne, and to the Lamb!" . . . Then one of the elders asked me, "These dressed in long white robes—who are they and where have they come from?" So I said to him, "My lord, you know the answer." Then he said to me, "These are the ones who have come out of the great

> tribulation. They have washed their robes and made them white in the blood of the Lamb!" (Rev 7:9–10, 13–14, cf. the parenthetical description of the rapture in Rev 14:14–16).

The Day of the Lord's Wrath

On the same day the rapture occurs, the day of the Lord's wrath begins, just as in the days of Noah and Lot (Luke 17:22–37, cf. 2 Thess 1:5–10). The onset of God's judgment is portrayed at the breaking of the seventh seal.

> Now when the Lamb opened the seventh seal there was silence in heaven for about half an hour. Then I saw the seven angels who stand before God, and seven trumpets were given to them. Another angel holding a golden censer came and was stationed at the altar. A large amount of incense was given to him to offer up, with the prayers of all the saints, on the golden altar that is before the throne. The smoke coming from the incense, along with the prayers of the saints, ascended before God from the angel's hand. Then the angel took the censer, filled it with fire from the altar, and threw it on the earth, and there were crashes of thunder, roaring, flashes of lightning, and an earthquake. Now the seven angels holding the seven trumpets prepared to blow them (Rev 8:1–6).

After this overture to the day of the Lord's wrath, the systematic elements of judgment begin in the execution of the trumpet and bowl judgments (Rev 8–9, 15–16). The prophets describe this period as righteous judgment, vengeful, fiery, dreadful, inescapable, bloody, destructive, and decisive (e.g. Joel 2:28–3:21, Isa 2:10–22, 13:6–13, Obad 15, Zeph 1:1–18). Jesus, Paul, and Peter warn that these judgments are for the wicked after God delivers his people (Matt 24:37–41, 1 Thess 5:1–11, 2 Pet 3:1–18).

In summary, the church will first experience the Antichrist's great tribulation, which will be cut short by the return of Christ to resurrect and rapture believers. Then the rapture will be followed immediately—on the same day—by the onset of the day of the Lord's wrath executed upon the ungodly. Considering this sober teaching, it is imperative that we spiritually prepare our hearts to be "overcomers" for what may soon come to pass, because Jesus warned: "Remember, I have told you ahead of time" (Matt 24:25).

Appendix 2

CHURCH MYSTERIES EXTEND INTO THE SEVENTIETH WEEK

I want to respond to a peculiar pretribulation argument that is sometimes used to separate Israel's program from the time of the church's program. It is believed that because certain "church mysteries" (i.e. various church doctrines) are missing from the Old Testament, this is evidence that the church will not exist simultaneously with Israel on earth during Daniel's seventieth week.[1] This theological-hermeneutic objection, however, does not work for the following reasons.

Mystery of the Resurrection of Living Saints

Let me begin with the most cited example. Contrary to pretribulation thought, the rapture is never called a "mystery" when believers are caught up to the sky to meet Jesus at his Parousia. Further, the resurrection is not a mystery, which was prophesied in the Old Testament concerning *dead* saints (Dan 12:2, Isa 26:19). The rapture was first prophesied during

1. E.g. Stanton, *Kept from the Hour*, 267; The Greek term *mystērion* means "the content of that which has not been known before but which has been revealed to an in-group or restricted constituency" and rendered as *secret* or *mystery* (LN).

the old covenant dispensation (John 14:1–4). Paul reveals that the mystery is where a generation of *living* saints will not have to die before they receive their glorious bodies when Christ returns: "Listen, I will tell you a mystery: We will not all sleep [die], but we will all be changed—in a moment, in the blinking of an eye, at the last trumpet. For the trumpet will sound, and the dead will be raised imperishable, and we will be changed" (1 Cor 15:51–52). Paul locates this event at the beginning of Jesus's Parousia (1 Cor 15:23, cf. 1 Thess 4:15). Jesus places the Parousia after (not before) the great tribulation (Matt 24:27, cf. 24:28–31). Consequently, pretribulationists are forced to construe *two* separate Parousia events so as not to place the rapture during the seventieth week.

In the remaining part of the appendix, I will outline other New Testament mysteries, which we will see transgress *into* the seventieth week and are fulfilled during that period or at its completion.

Mystery of the Olive Tree

> For if you were cut off from what is by nature a wild olive tree, and grafted, contrary to nature, into a cultivated olive tree, how much more will these natural branches be grafted back into their own olive tree? For I do not want you to be ignorant of this *mystery*, brothers and sisters, so that you may not be conceited: A partial hardening has happened to Israel **[during the church age]** until the full number of the Gentiles has come in. And so all Israel will be saved, as it is written: "The Deliverer will come out of Zion; he will remove ungodliness from Jacob. And this is my covenant with them, when I take away their sins **[at the completion of the seventieth week]**" (Rom 11:24–27, cf. 1:1–2, 16:25–26, Col 1:26–27, cf. Dan 9:24–27).

Mystery of Lawlessness

> For the *mystery* of lawlessness is already at work **[during the church age]**; only he who now restrains will do so until he is taken out of the way **[at the midpoint of the seventieth week]** (2 Thess 2:7).

Mystery of the Kingdom

> Jesus answered them, "To you it has been granted to know the *mysteries* of the kingdom of heaven **[during the church age]** . . . . and the harvest is the end of the age, and the reapers are angels. So just as the tares are gathered up and burned with fire, so shall it be at the end of the age **[at a point during the second half of the seventieth week]**" (Matt 13:11, 39–40 NASB, cf. 24:14, 28:20).[2]

Mystery of God

> But in the days when the seventh angel is about to blow

---

2. These kingdom illustrations refer to the period of the church age during which the gospel is proclaimed. These illustrations include: sowing seeds (Matt 13:3–9, 18–30, cf. 36–43); the mustard seed growing into a tree (Matt 13:31–32); leaven in the flour (Matt 13:33); a treasure (Matt 13:44); a pearl of great value (Matt 13:45–46); and good and bad fish (Matt 13:47–50). There are other teachings from the Gospels during the old covenant dispensation in which Jesus illustrates that the church age was in the plan of God before Israel's rejection: confession of Jesus as Messiah builds the church (Matt 16:18); church discipline (Matt 18:17); and incorporation of Gentiles into the new covenant community (John 10:16); the rapture of the church (John 14:1–4); the coming of the Holy Spirit (John 14:15–31). Finally, it suffices to give a few examples of Old Testament prophetic passages that signal the coming church age: Christ's session in heaven (Ps 110:1, cf. Acts 2:34–35); the period of Israel's worldwide dispersion (Deut 30:1–7); the times between Jesus's crucifixion in AD 33 and Jerusalem's destruction in AD 70 (Dan 9:26–27) (Gundry, *Church and the Tribulation*, 14–18). All of these examples further demonstrate that there is no necessary theological principle for the church to be excluded from the predicted time of Israel's last seven years of rebellion.

> his trumpet, the *mystery* of God **[happening during the church age]** is completed **[the end of the seventieth week]**, just as he has proclaimed to his servants the prophets (Rev 10:7).[3]

Mystery of Babylon the Great

> On her forehead was written a name, a *mystery*: "Babylon the Great, the Mother of prostitutes and of the detestable things of the earth" (Rev 17:5).

Regarding this last instance of a mystery, there is a link between Babylon the Great's persecution and the Bride. Babylon is responsible for the martyrdom of many saints (Rev 18:24—19:2), who are identified as part of the bride:

> Then I heard what sounded like the voice of a vast throng, like the roar of many waters and like loud crashes of thunder. *They* were shouting: "Hallelujah! For the Lord our God, the All-Powerful, reigns! Let us rejoice and exult

3. The identification of the "mystery of God" is not explicit here. A full explanation is outside the scope of discussion; however, there are a couple of reasons to believe that the completion of the partial hardening of Israel and her final eschatological salvation is in view, including the full number of Gentiles. In the immediate context, the completion of the mystery is said to occur "in the days when the seventh angel is about to blow his trumpet." The blowing of the seventh trumpet occurs at the completion of the seventieth week. This passage is part of a larger parenthetical section that references the last half of Daniel's seventieth week (Rev 11:2–3). We know that the original purpose for the seventy weeks was to determine how long the Gentiles would dominate Israel, a time after which God would bring salvation to Israel (Dan 9:24–27). In addition, Paul calls the salvation of Israel a "mystery" in which the fulfillment occurs when the Messiah returns. This includes the full number of Gentiles (Rom 11:24–26). Accordingly, the "mystery of God" that was "proclaimed to his servants the prophets" likely refers to the salvation of Israel as well as the Gentiles. Not surprisingly, this occurs in the context of the kingdom of Christ reverting back to him: "Then the seventh angel blew his trumpet, and there were loud voices in heaven saying: 'The kingdom of the world has become the kingdom of our Lord and of his Christ, and he will reign for ever and ever'" (Rev 11:15, cf. Rev 10:7).

> and give him glory, because the wedding celebration of the Lamb has come, and his *bride* has made herself ready. She was permitted to be dressed in bright, clean, fine linen" (for the fine linen is the righteous deeds of the *saints*). Then the angel said to me, "Write the following: Blessed are those who are invited to the banquet at the wedding celebration of the Lamb!" He also said to me, "These are the true words of God" (Rev 19:6–9).

In Rev 13:7, the saints are described as having the status of suffering as the object of persecution by the Beast: "The beast was permitted to go to war against the saints and conquer them. He was given ruling authority over every tribe, people, language, and nation." The saints are later described as the bride of Christ with the privileged status of participating in the wedding celebration in Rev 19:7-8. During the seventieth week, the "mystery" of Babylon the Great involves killing members of the bride that clearly must take place on earth, not in heaven.

In summary, instances of mysteries give additional support that the church will exist on earth as she enters the seventieth week of Daniel. The church age, then, will not cease when the seventieth week begins. This mystery thread of evidence argues that God will be active with the church alongside Israel during the seventieth week.[4]

4. There are other mysteries occurring during the present church period that will extend into Daniel's seventieth week; e.g. Col 2:2–3, 1 Tim 3:16, Eph 1:9–10; cf. Gundry, *Church and the Tribulation*, 13–14.

Bibliography

Akin, Danny. "A Rapture You Can't Miss." Pages 46–61 in *The Return of Christ: A Premillennial Perspective*. Edited by David L. Allen and Steve W. Lemke. Nashville: B&H Academic, 2011.

Bigalke Ron J., Jr., ed. *Progressive Dispensationalism: An Analysis of the Movement and Defense of Traditional Dispensationalism*. Lanham, MD: University of Press of America, 2005.

Blaising, Craig A. "A Case for the Pretribulation Rapture." Pages 25–73 in *Three Views on the Rapture: Pretribulation, Prewrath, or Posttribulation*. Edited by Alan Hultberg. 2nd ed. Grand Rapids: Zondervan, 2010.

———. "Dispensationalism: The Search for Definition." Pages 13–34 in *Dispensationalism, Israel, and the Church*. Edited by Craig A. Blaising and Darrell L. Bock. Grand Rapids: Zondervan, 1992.

———. "A Pretribulation Response." Pages 155–67 in *Three Views on the Rapture: Pretribulation, Prewrath, or Posttribulation*. Edited by Alan Hultberg. Grand Rapids: Zondervan, 2010.

Blaising, Craig A., and Darrell L. Bock. *Progressive Dispensationalism*. Wheaton, IL: BridgePoint, 1993.

Blomberg, Craig L. *The Historical Reliability of the Gospels*. 2nd ed. Downers Grove, IL: IVP Academic, 2007.

Brindle, Wayne A. "Biblical Evidence for the Imminence of the Rapture." *Bibliotheca Sacra* 158 (2001): 138–51.

Brumett, John. "Does Progressive Dispensationalism Teach a Posttribulational Rapture?" Pages 285–306 in *Progressive Dispensationalism: An Analysis of the Movement and Defense of Traditional Dispensationalism*. Edited by Ron J. Bigalke, Jr. Lanham, MD: University of Press of America, 2005.

Cameron, Robert. *Scriptural Truth about the Lord's Return*. New York: Revell, 1922.

Carson, D. A. *Exegetical Fallacies*. 2nd ed. Grand Rapids: Baker, 1996.

Chafer, Lewis Sperry. *Major Bible Themes*. Chicago: Moody, 1942.

———. *Systematic Theology*. 8 vols. Dallas, TX: Dallas Seminary Press, 1947–1948.

Cooper, Charles. "Dispensational Foundations: Acts, Joel, and Revelation, Part 2 of 2." *Parousia* 7 (1998): 2–8.

———. *God's Elect and the Great Tribulation: An Interpretation of Matthew 24:1–31 and Daniel 9*. Bellefonte, PA: Strong Tower Publishing, 2008.

———. "Theological Winds of Change: Significance for the Rapture Question, Part 1 of 2." *Parousia* 6 (1998): 2–8.

Cosby, Michael R. "Hellenistic Formal Receptions and Paul's use of ΑΠΑΝΤΗΣΙΣ in 1 Thessalonians 4.17." *Bulletin for Biblical Research* 4 (1994): 15–34.

Darby, John Nelson. *The Collected Writings of J. N. Darby*. Vol. 11. Edited by William Kelly. Oak Park, IL: Bible Truth Publishers, 1962.

———. *Letters of J. N. Darby Volume One: 1832–1868*. Reprint. Oak Park, IL: Bible Truth Publishers, 1971.

Elmore, Floyd. "J. N. Darby's Early Years." Pages 127–150 in *When the Trumpet Sounds*. Edited by Thomas Ice and Timothy Demy. Eugene, OR: Harvest House, 1995.

Feinberg, John S. "Arguing for the Rapture: Who Must Prove What and How?" Pages 187–210 in *When the Trumpet Sounds*. Edited by Thomas Ice and Timothy Demy. Eugene, OR: Harvest House, 1995.

Feinberg, Paul D. "The Case for the Pretribulation Rapture Position." Pages 45–86 in *Three Views on the Rapture:*

Pre-, Mid-, or Post-Tribulational? Grand Rapids: Zondervan, 1984.

———. "Response: Paul D. Feinberg." Pages 147–58 in *Three Views on the Rapture: Pre-, Mid-, or Post-Tribulational?* Grand Rapids: Zondervan, 1984.

Fowler, C. L. *Building the Dispensations.* Denver, CO: Maranatha Publications, 1940.

Frederick W. Danker, Walter Bauer, William F. Arndt, and F. Wilbur Gingrich. *A Greek-English Lexicon of the New Testament and Other Early Christian Literature.* 3rd ed. Chicago: University of Chicago Press, 2000 (BDAG).

Fruchtenbaum, Arnold G. "Is There a Pre-Wrath Rapture?" Pages 381–411 in *When the Trumpet Sounds.* Edited by Thomas Ice and Timothy Demy. Eugene, OR: Harvest House, 1995.

Gaebelein, Arno C. *The Harmony of the Prophetic Word.* New York: Our Hope, 1907.

Gundry, Robert H. *The Church and the Tribulation: A Biblical Examination of Posttribulationism.* Grand Rapids: Zondervan, 1973.

———. *First the Antichrist: Why Christ Won't Come Before the Antichrist Does.* Grand Rapids: Baker, 1997.

Hart, John F. "Jesus and the Rapture: Matthew 24." Pages 45–71 in *Evidence for the Rapture: A Biblical Case for Pretribulationism.* Edited by John F. Hart. Chicago: Moody, 2015.

———. "Should Pretribulationists Reconsider the Rapture in Matthew 24:36–44, Part 1 of 3." *The Journal of the Grace Evangelical Society* 20 (2007): 47–70.

Hindson, Edward E. "The Rapture and the Return: Two Aspects of Christ's Coming." Pages 151–62 in *When the Trumpet Sounds.* Edited by Thomas Ice and Timothy Demy. Eugene, OR: Harvest House, 1995.

Hitchcock, Mark. *Could the Rapture Happen Today?* Sisters, OR: Multnomah Publishers, 2005.

Hoehner, Harold W. *Chronological Aspects of the Life of Christ*. Grand Rapids: Zondervan, 1977.

House, Wayne. "Dangers of Progressive Dispensationalism to Premillennial Theology: Reflections of a Pre-Progressive Dispensationalist." Pages 327–41 in *Progressive Dispensationalism: An Analysis of the Movement and Defense of Traditional Dispensationalism*. Edited by Ron J. Bigalke, Jr. Lanham, MD: University of Press of America, 2005.

Hoyt, Herman A. *The End Times*. Chicago: Moody Press, 1969.

Huebner, R. A. *J. N. Darby's Teaching Regarding Dispensations, Ages, Administrations and the Two Parentheses*. Morganville, NJ: Present Truth Publishers, 1993.

Hultberg, Alan, ed. *Three Views on the Rapture: Pretribulationism, Prewrath, Or Posttribulationism*. 2nd ed. Grand Rapids: Zondervan, 2010.

Ironside, Henry A. *Expository Notes on the Epistles of James and Peter*. New York: Loizeaux Brothers, 1947.

Karleen, Paul S. *The Pre-Wrath Rapture of the Church: Is It Biblical?* Langhorne, PA: BF Press, 1991.

Kline, Meredith G. "Primal Parousia." *Westminster Theological Journal* 40 (1978): 245–80.

Koehler, Ludwig, Walter Baumgartner, and Johann J. Stamm. *The Hebrew and Aramaic Lexicon of the Old Testament*. Translated and edited under the supervision of Mervyn E. J. Richardson. 4 vols. Leiden: Brill, 1994–1999 (HALOT).

Kreider, Glenn R. "The Rapture and the Day of the Lord." Pages 73–97 in *Evidence for the Rapture: A Biblical Case for Pretribulationism*. Edited by John F. Hart. Chicago: Moody, 2015.

Kreitzer, L. J. *Jesus and God in Paul's Eschatology*. Journal for the Study of the New Testament: Supplement Series 19; Sheffield: JSOT Press, 1987.

Kurschner, Alan. *Antichrist Before the Day of the Lord: What Every Christian Needs to Know about the Return of*

Christ. Pompton Lakes, NJ: Eschatos Publishing, 2013.

———. "James Barr on the 'Illegitimate Totality Transfer' Word-Concept Fallacy." Pages 70–89 in *James Barr Assessed: Evaluating His Legacy over the Last Sixty Years*. Edited by Stanley E. Porter. Biblical Interpretation Series 192. Leiden: Brill, 2021.

———. *A Linguistic Approach to Revelation 19:11–20:6 and the Millennium Binding of Satan*. Linguistic Biblical Studies 23. Leiden: Brill, 2022.

Kurschner, Alan and Michael J. Svigel. "Who Sat on the Thrones in Revelation 20:4? Ἐκάθισαν and Its Implications." Paper presented at the Evangelical Theological Society Annual Meeting. Fort Worth, TX, 17 November 2021.

Ladd, George Eldon. *The Blessed Hope: A Biblical Study on the Second Advent and the Rapture*. Grand Rapids: MI: Eerdmans, 1956.

LaHaye, Tim. "Twelve Reasons Why This Could Be the Terminal Generation." Pages 427–44 in *When the Trumpet Sounds*. Edited by Thomas Ice and Timothy Demy. Eugene, OR: Harvest House, 1995.

Lewis, Stephen R. "The New Covenant: Enacted or Ratified." Pages 135–43 in *Progressive Dispensationalism: An Analysis of the Movement and Defense of Traditional Dispensationalism*. Edited by Ron J. Bigalke, Jr. Lanham, MD: University of Press of America, 2005.

Louw, J. P., and E. A. Nida. *Greek-English Lexicon of the New Testament Based on Semantic Domains*. 2 vols. New York: United Bible Societies, 1988 (LN).

MacArthur, John "Is Christ's Return Imminent?" *The Master's Seminary Journal* 11 (2000): 7–18.

———. *Revelation 1–11*. MacArthur New Testament Commentary Series 32. Chicago: Moody, 1999.

Mathewson, David L. *Revelation: A Handbook on the Greek Text*. Baylor Handbook on the Greek New Testament. Waco, TX: Baylor University Press, 2016.

Mangum, R. Todd, and Mark S. Sweetnam. *The Scofield Bible:*

Its History and Impact on the Evangelical Church. Colorado Springs, CO: Paternoster, 2009.

Mayhue, Richard L. "The Bible's Watchword: Day of the Lord." *The Master's Seminary Journal* 22 (2011): 65–88.

——. "Why A Pretribulation Rapture?" Pages 85–102 in *Christ's Prophetic Plans: A Futuristic Premillennial Primer.* Edited by John MacArthur and Richard Mayhue. Chicago: Moody, 2012.

McLean, John A. "Another Look at Rosenthal's 'Pre-Wrath Rapture.'" *Bibilotheca Sacra* 148 (1991): 388–98.

Mealy, J. Webb. *After the Thousand Years: Resurrection and Judgment in Revelation* 20. Journal for the Study of the New Testament: Supplement Series 70. Sheffield: Journal for the Study of the Old Testament Press, 1991.

Moo, Douglas J. "A Case for the Posttribulation Rapture." Pages 186–241 in *Three Views on the Rapture: Pretribulationism, Prewrath, Or Posttribulationism.* Edited by Alan Hultberg. 2nd ed. Grand Rapids: Zondervan, 2010.

Morris, Benny. *1948: A History of the First Arab-Israel War.* New Haven, Yale University Press, 2008.

Mounce, Robert, H. *The Book of Revelation.* Revised ed., The New International Commentary on the New Testament. Grand Rapids: Eerdmans, 1997.

Nicholl, Colin R. *From Hope to Despair in Thessalonica: Situating 1 and 2 Thessalonians.* SNTSMS 126. Cambridge: Cambridge University Press, 2004.

Niehaus, Jeffrey J. *God at Sinai: Covenant & Theophany in the Bible and Ancient Near East.* Grand Rapids, MI: Zondervan, 1995.

Olander David E. "The Pre-Day of the Lord Rapture." Pages 269–91 in *Dispensationalism Tomorrow and Beyond: A Theological Collection in Honor of Charles C. Ryrie.* Edited by Christopher Cone. Fort Worth, TX: Tyndale Seminary Press, 2008.

Parle, Joseph. *Dispensational Development and Departure:*

Comparing Classical, Essentialist, and Progressive Dispensational Models. Lee's Summit, MO: Exegetical Publishing, 2020.

Patterson, Paige. "Israel and the Great Tribulation." Pages 62–74 in *The Return of Christ: A Premillennial Perspective*. Edited by David L. Allen and Steve W. Lemke. Nashville: B&H Academic, 2011.

Pentecost, J. Dwight. *Things to Come: A Study in Biblical Eschatology*. Grand Rapids: Zondervan, 1958.

Pettegrew, Larry D. "The Rapture Debate at the Niagara Bible Conference." *Bibliotheca Sacra* 157 (2000): 331–47.

Porter, Stanley E. and Alan E. Kurschner, eds. *The Future Restoration of Israel: A Response to Supersessionism*. McMaster General Studies Series. Eugene, OR: Pickwick (forthcoming).

Reiter, Richard R. "A History of the Development of the Rapture Positions." Pages 11–44 in *Three Views on the Rapture: Pre-, Mid-, or Post-Tribulational?* Grand Rapids: Zondervan, 1984.

Roller, O. "Das Buch mit sieben Siegeln." *Zeitschrift für die neutestamentliche Wissenschaft und die Kunde der älteren Kirche* 36 (1937): 98–113.

Rosenthal, Marvin. *The Pre-Wrath Rapture of the Church*. Nashville: Nelson, 1990.

Rydelnik, Michael A. "Israel: Why the Church Must Be Raptured Before the Tribulation." Pages 255–76 in *Evidence for the Rapture: A Biblical Case for Pretribulationism*. Edited by John F. Hart. Chicago: Moody, 2015.

Ryrie, Charles C. *The Basis of the Premillennial Faith*. Neptune, NJ: Loizeaux Brothers, 1953.

———. *Come Quickly, Lord Jesus: What You Need to Know about the Rapture*. Revised. Eugene, OR: Harvest House, 1996.

———. *Dispensationalism Today*. Chicago: Moody Press, 1965.

———. *Dispensationalism*. Revised ed. Chicago: Moody Press,

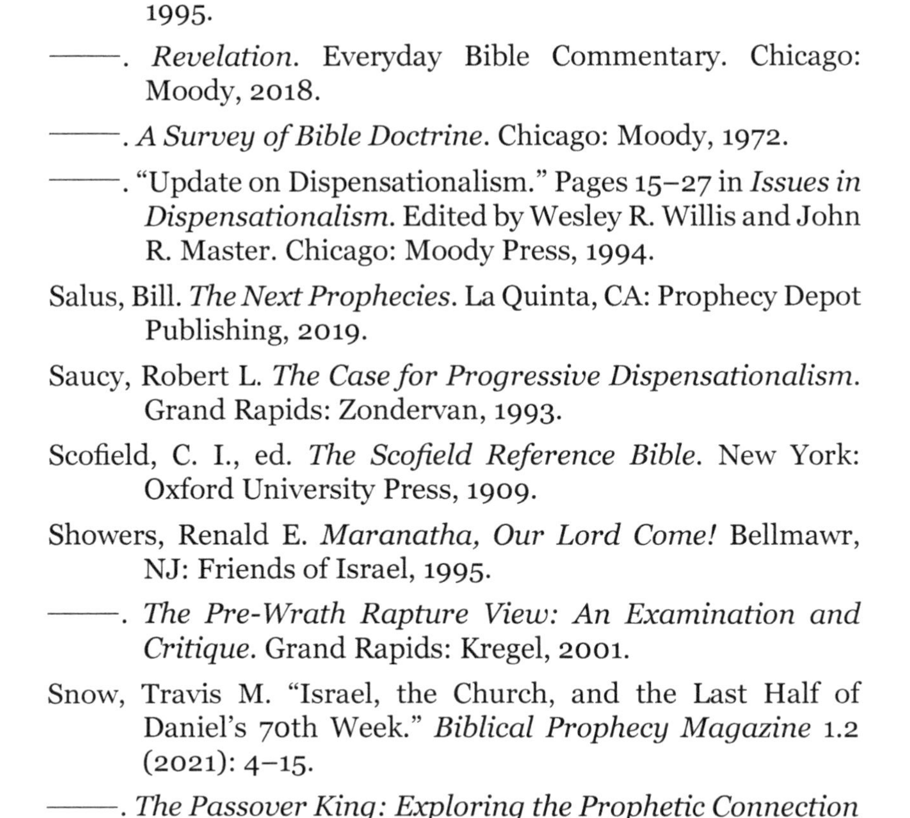

1995.

———. *Revelation*. Everyday Bible Commentary. Chicago: Moody, 2018.

———. *A Survey of Bible Doctrine*. Chicago: Moody, 1972.

———. "Update on Dispensationalism." Pages 15–27 in *Issues in Dispensationalism*. Edited by Wesley R. Willis and John R. Master. Chicago: Moody Press, 1994.

Salus, Bill. *The Next Prophecies*. La Quinta, CA: Prophecy Depot Publishing, 2019.

Saucy, Robert L. *The Case for Progressive Dispensationalism*. Grand Rapids: Zondervan, 1993.

Scofield, C. I., ed. *The Scofield Reference Bible*. New York: Oxford University Press, 1909.

Showers, Renald E. *Maranatha, Our Lord Come!* Bellmawr, NJ: Friends of Israel, 1995.

———. *The Pre-Wrath Rapture View: An Examination and Critique*. Grand Rapids: Kregel, 2001.

Snow, Travis M. "Israel, the Church, and the Last Half of Daniel's 70th Week." *Biblical Prophecy Magazine* 1.2 (2021): 4–15.

———. *The Passover King: Exploring the Prophetic Connection between Passover, the End Times, and the Return of Jesus*. Dallas, TX: Voice of Messiah, 2020.

Sproule, John A. *In Defense of Pretribulationism*. Winona Lake, IN: BMH Books, 1980.

———. *Twelve Sermons on the Second Coming of Christ*. Grand Rapids: Baker, 1976.

Stallard, Mike, ed. *Dispensational Understanding of the New Covenant*. Schaumburg, IL: Regular Baptist Books, 2012.

———. "What Do Israel and the Church Share from a Traditional Dispensational Viewpoint?" Paper presented at the Council on Dispensational Hermeneutics. Clarks Summit, PA, 16-17 Sept 2015.

Stanton, Gerald B. "The Doctrine of Imminency: Is It Biblical?" Pages 221–33 in *When the Trumpet Sounds*. Edited by Thomas Ice and Timothy Demy. Eugene, OR: Harvest House, 1995.

———. *Kept from the Hour: Biblical Evidence for the Pretribulational Return of Christ*. Miami Spring, FL: Schoettle Publishing, 1991.

Tanner, J. Paul. *Daniel*. Evangelical Exegetical Commentary. Bellingham, WA: Lexham Press, 2020.

Thomas, Robert L. "1, 2 Thessalonians." In *Expositor's Bible Commentary*. Edited by Frank E. Gaebelein, vol 11. Grand Rapids: Zondervan, 1978.

———. "The Hermeneutics of Progressive Dispensationalism." Pages 1–15 in *Progressive Dispensationalism: An Analysis of the Movement and Defense of Traditional Dispensationalism*. Edited by Ron J. Bigalke, Jr. Lanham, MD: University of Press of America, 2005.

———. "Imminence In the NT, Especially Paul's Thessalonians Epistles." *The Master's Seminary Journal* 13 (2002): 191–214.

———. "The Place of Imminence in Recent Eschatological Systems." Pages 199–216 in *Looking into the Future: Evangelical Studies in Eschatology*. Edited by David W. Baker. Grand Rapids: Baker, 2001.

———. "The Rapture and the Biblical Teaching of Imminency." Pages 23–43 in *Evidence for the Rapture: A Biblical Case for Pretribulationism*. Edited by John F. Hart. Chicago: Moody, 2015.

Tregelles, S. P. *The Hope of Christ's Second Coming: How Is it Taught in Scripture? And Why?* London: Houlston & Wright, 1864.

Van Kampen, Robert D. *The Sign*. 2nd ed. Wheaton, IL: Crossway, 1999.

Walvoord, John F. "Is Daniel's Seventieth Week Future?" *Bibliotheca Sacra* 101 (1944): 30–49.

———. *The Rapture Question*. Findlay, OH: Dunham Publishing, 1957.

———. *The Rapture Question*. Revised. Grand Rapids, MI: Zondervan, 1979.

———. *The Revelation of Jesus Christ*. Chicago: Moody, 1989.

Zuber, Kevin, D. "Paul and the Rapture: 1 Thessalonians 4–5." Pages 145–72 in *Evidence for the Rapture: A Biblical Case for Pretribulationism*. Edited by John F. Hart. Chicago: Moody, 2015.

Scripture Index

Mark

Luke

2 Thessalonians

CPSIA information can be obtained
at www.ICGtesting.com
Printed in the USA
JSHW052318051122
R12049600001B/R120496PG32522JSX00001B/1

9 780985 363390